REGIONAL ANALYSIS AND THE NEW INTERNATIONAL DIVISION OF LABOR

STUDIES IN APPLIED REGIONAL SCIENCE

REGIONAL ANALYSIS AND THE NEW INTERNATIONAL DIVISION OF LABOR
Applications of a Political Economy Approach

Edited By

FRANK MOULAERT
Katholieke Universiteit
Leuven, Belgium
and
PATRICIA WILSON SALINAS
University of Texas
Austin, Texas

FOREWORD BY
JOHN FRIEDMAN

KLUWER•NIJHOFF PUBLISHING
Boston The Hague London

Distributors for North America:
Kluwer•Nijhoff Publishing
Kluwer Boston, Inc.
190 Old Derby Street
Hingham, Massachusetts 02043, U.S.A.

Distributors outside North America:
Kluwer Academic Publishers Group
Distribution Centre
P.O. Box 322
3300AH Dordrecht, The Netherlands

Library of Congress Cataloging in Publication Data
Main entry under title:

Regional analysis and the new international division of labor.
(Studies in applied regional science)
Bibliography: p.
Includes index.
1. International economic relations—Addresses, essays, lectures. 2. Regional economics—Addresses, essays, lectures. 3. Space in economics—Addresses, essays, lectures. I. Moulaert, Frank. II. Salinas, Patricia Wilson. III. Series.
HF141.R418 338'.06 82-15342
ISBN-13: 978-94-009-7411-1 e-ISBN-13: 978-94-009-7409-8
DOI: 10.1007/978-94-009-7409-8

Aan Greet
and
To Nelson

First versions of most of the chapters in this book were presented at the sessions on 'Regional Political Economy' at the first world conference of the World University (held at Harvard University, Cambridge, USA, June 6–June 23 1980). These sessions were organized by the editors with the support of Dr. Walter Isard. We wish to thank him for this.

CONTENTS

Foreword

Throughout the world, a sense of crisis has settled in like a nightmare that refuses to leave. We look towards the horizon with apprehension. Major changes are afoot. Older industrial regions, once rich and powerful, stand by helplessly as factories close down. Poor countries are sliding into bankruptcy, unable even to feed their populations. In a few scattered enclaves, called export platforms, new manufacturing plants spring up overnight: they employ predominantly young, unmarried women and ship their products to unknown destinations overseas. Small companies are eaten up by bigger ones which, in turn, are absorbed by still larger conglomerates. Some industrial sectors are wiped out altogether. Tensions between states are increasing. More and more countries are coming under military rule. Torture and terrorism are turned into tools of official state policy. Civil wars are fought in Central America, Northern Africa, and Southeast Asia. International conflict flares up between Britain and Argentina, Iraq and Iran, Ethiopia and Somalia. Economic growth has slowed to a crawl. Inflation undercuts the livelihood of the poor. The small producer is ruined.

It appears that we are involved in a major restructuring of the capitalist world. The problems are profits, capital accumulation, and efficiency in production. To make the indicators point up, whole regions are sacrificed, new technologies are put in place, and new locational patterns are created as the world is carved up into a new international division of labor. A few giant corporations and financial institutions, holding the bulk of the available capital, are making the strategic decisions. For the first time in history, production, distribution, and finance are being organized and managed on a global scale. Even socialist countries are drawn into this network: China is building export platforms of her own, the Soviet Union has become a major food importer, and smaller socialist countries, such as Poland and Yugoslavia, are deeply in debt to transnational capital.

During the last decade or so, political economy has become the most adequate theoretical mode of inquiry into this process of restructuring and crisis. As Frank Moulaert explains in chapter 2, there are dramatic differences between the explanatory models of political economy and those of neoclassical economics that they replace. Neoclassical economics looks towards the harmonization of the system of economic relatons; they describe a state of equilibrium. Political economy models, on the other hand, seek to account for change and movement. Their point of reference is history and the struggles that animate it. These struggles are political in nature, and they take various forms: between social classes; between fractions of a class; between regional class-alliances and the state; between states. They are fought for different reasons, but mostly for material interests and power.

Central to all these struggles is the state, the political apparatus of a country. Political economy has long sought to clarify the role of the state. How much autonomy does it have? In whose interests does it act? The answers are not without ambiguity, and it is unlikely that a general theory of the state can ever be formulated. States, after all, are historical constructs and are themselves in flux. Despite this, a few things can be said that appear to be valid for the countries dominated by the capitalist mode of production. States must walk a thin line between serving capital and their own interests in maintaining legitimate rule. The more they serve the former, the greater are the dangers of delegitimization. The more legitimate authority is put in question, the greater will be the state's recourse to brute power and the suppression of political opposition.

The political economy approach is especially valuable for regional studies. Regions, as Ann Markusen reminds us, are not artifacts. They define themselves in political action. The present crisis has discrete and variable effects on regional populations and territorially organized political systems. People respond to these effects in different ways. New coalitions are formed, for instance, between community and labor. A see-saw battle is being waged over the distribution of effective political power to control the movements of capital. Overall, the tendency appears to be towards a greater decentralization of power to provincial and local levels. It is essentially a defensive strategy that reasserts a political will in the face of economic power. The relation is a mutually limiting one, for neither regions nor capital can go it alone. Only this much is clear: the inherited system of state power is itself in crisis and will emerge greatly altered from the present struggles. A new world is being forged.

The book provides us with an excellent introduction to the political economy of regional struggles. It bears very little resemblance to essay collections of a few years ago, which still bear the neoclassical imprint. Political economy addresses a different set of problems and explicitly introduces the role of social movements and the state into the analysis. This book is appropriately international not only in its coverage but in the national background of the authors. English, American, Argentinian, Belgian, French, and Greek – few of them seem to be working in the country in which they were born, which in itself underscores the globalization of economic relations.

The text should be read as an introduction to the subject and to the method of analysis. The book does not pretend to be a definitive treatment – indeed, political economy is full of lively controversy. As the chapters by Coraggio and Markusen show, these controversies are by no means trivial and lead to major differences in emphasis and interpretation.

Throughout this book, the state is treated in a relatively passive way as the arena of class struggle. But other possibilities are entertained that assign a more active role to the state. But on whose side? This, too, is in contention, as some argue for greater state autonomy, while others see the state primarily as an instrument of class domination. Which version one adopts is important for practice. Are reforms possible? Are they even desirable? How militant should practice be? Can power be shared? Are compromises possible? In what ways should policy questions be addressed?

Political economists may not wish to advise an increasingly authoritarian state, but they cannot afford the luxury of not giving any advice whatsoever. This, it seems to me, is the challenge that lies beyond this book. Practice is central to the validation of knowledge, in political economy no less than engineering. Political economists must move beyond analysis to the study of appropriate forms of political practice, to specific strategies for democratic change. This book is a first and necessary step in that direction.

John Friedmann
Professor of Urban and Regional Planning
University of California
Los Angeles

REGIONAL ANALYSIS AND THE NEW INTERNATIONAL DIVISION OF LABOR

1 REGIONAL POLITICAL ECONOMY
An Introduction and Overview

Patricia Wilson Salinas and Frank Moulaert

Regional analysis – the study of human activity over geographic space – has been guided predominantly by neoclassical economics, with an added spatial or geographic dimension. Walter Isard formalized this mode of regional analysis in the 1950s, under the name *regional science*.[1] More recently, another approach to regional analysis has emerged – with its roots in classical political economy rather than neoclassical economics.[2] It was developed largely during the 1970s, under the name *regional political economy*.

This book brings together carefully selected contributions to the literature on regional political economy. Designed as an interlocking set of essays, its main purpose is to show the applicability of regional political economy, not just in describing the most recent changes in the spatial organization of production in the United States, Europe, and developing countries, but in explaining the root causes of these changes. Specifically, these spatial changes are linked to changes in the international division of labor – that is, the reorganization of production on an integrated global scale, which dictates new roles for national and subnational economies.

To highlight the unique contribution of the literature of regional political economy in explaining these changes, the first part of the book contrasts the theories, concepts, and methodologies used in regional political economy and regional science. The remainder of the book provides case studies from the United States, Europe, and developing countries. The main contributions of each chapter are summarized in this chapter, following a brief overview of the basic concepts of regional political economy.

An Introduction to Regional Political Economy

The regional scientist views spatial analysis as a highly specialized examination of one aspect of social behavior – especially economic behavior. The regional political economist explains spatial organization as a manifestation of the logic of the social system itself. The logic of a social system lies in its manner of organizing the production and distribution of wealth, which results in a particular pattern of social relations of production that are typically hierarchical. The regional political economist analyzes the needs and motives of the dominant social groups, their struggles to maintain and increase their dominance, the struggles by the dominated groups against the more powerful ones, and the effect of these struggles on spatial organization. This analysis is based on the following conceptualization of social structure and social change.[3]

The first task of humankind is to survive and reproduce. The struggle of humanity against nature reflects this task. Humans must produce sufficient goods (food, shelter, and other socially determined necessities) to survive the struggle against nature. This survival necessitates a social organization of production, called the *mode of production*. The mode of production is characterized by the form of social control over the means of production (natural resources and the tools with which people transform the natural resources for their own purposes), which gives rise to a particular pattern of social relations. The mode of production is also shaped by the level of technological development of the productive forces (labor and means of production).

When the level of development of the productive forces is high enough, society produces more than the basic physical and social necessities of reproduction; in other words, a surplus is produced. Whenever a surplus is produced, a hierarchy in the social relations occurs according to who is able to appropriate the surplus.[4] This struggle is the basis of class conflict – the class that appropriates surplus (by controlling the means of production) versus the class that produces surplus (by working with the means of production).

Some social formations or social systems are composed of more than one mode of production. In such cases, an additional motivating force is present: the struggle between the principal appropriators (dominant class) of one mode of production and the appropriators of the other modes of production to gain more surplus and retain their hegemonic position.

To the three basic struggles in a social formation – humankind against nature, appropriating class versus producing class, and appropriating class of one mode of production against appropriating class of another – a fourth struggle of lesser importance may be added: rivalry within a class for control of surplus. To understand how these struggles are played out in any social formation is to understand the logic of the historical development of that society.

These struggles to appropriate and increase surplus occur not only in the productive system. Every social formation is composed of a productive base formed by the constituent modes of production and a superstructure composed of the social institutions – political, cultural, educational, and religious – and ideological values that reinforce the system of production and surplus appropriation. The struggle for surplus unfolds on the level of social and ideological superstructure as well as on the productive level. To understand any given social formation, the political economist identifies not only the various modes of production involved, the hierarchical relationship among them, and the class conflicts within them, but also the social and ideological superstructure of the social formation that reinforces the dominance of the upper class of the strongest mode over the lower classes of that mode and over the weaker modes.

To understand how those struggles to gain, maintain, and increase control over surplus operate over space is to understand the logic behind the development of spatial organization in a society. Spatial organization reflects those struggles and the underlying social relations of production.

Theory, Method, and the Concept of Region

In chapter 2, Frank Moulaert elaborates on the differences in method and theory between regional science and regional political economy, which are closely related to the world views held in each school. Moulaert explains that idealism is the basis of the world view behind neoclassical economics, which is the school of thought behind regional science. Idealists view the world as a free, harmonious society, where individuals attempt to maximize their satisfaction and in this way contribute to the general well-being. This idealistic view is in sharp contrast to the materialist view of a world full of contradiction, domination, and struggle, which typifies the political economy world view. This difference in world view between regional scientists and political economists explains many of their theoretical differences.

Moulaert characterizes the methodological differences between the two approaches as the contrast between regional science's positivism and regional political economy's dialectics. Positivism restricts itself to the study of the measurable aspects of relations between tangible, discernible elements. Dialectics deals with the dynamics of relations and elements within a dynamic structure, even if they are metaphysical or qualitative in nature. Thus, regional political economy attempts not to add more dimensions – for example, political, social, ideological – to regional science but to provide a different theoretical and methodological basis for understanding spatial organization.

The regional scientist views space as a determinant of interactions among economic and social actors, while the regional political economist, as Jose Luis Coraggio explains in chapter 3, views space as the locus of a set of social relations. The category *region* is relevant to the regional political economist primarily as it manifests the spaceness, or spatial organization, of the social relations of production. Note that this concept of space, as explained by Coraggio, does not exclude the physical or geological configuration as part of the spatial organization but considers it "as a factor that, within the given social process, orients the concrete territorial configuration... of social phenomena but in no way produces it."

Territorially defined regions are relevant to political economists when conflicts in social relations of production are perceived by the actors involved as regional conflicts. In chapter 4, Ann Markusen calls this perception *regionalism* – "the political claim of a territorially identified group of people against one or several mechanisms of the State. ... Although regionalism is clearly a subjective and experiential term, it may also refer to the objective social dynamics that cause territorial differences in social formations."

Because the term *region*, warns Markusen, "connotes a territorial, not social, entity," its use can lead to a number of analytical errors. First, region might be confused with the whole of social relations that are territorially based. As such, a class conflict or a conflict between cultural groups might be understood falsely as a conflict between regions (Markusen gives a number of examples). Second, it is very possible that the existing territorially defined regions are only partly relevant for the spaceness of the social relations determining the dynamics of social reality in the region. This is the case, for example, where the social relations are predominantly international or where, as in a primitive society, cultural alienation is a product of the import of Western life style.

Although Markusen explains very well when territorially defined regions can be an issue in political economy, a regional issue can only be fully understood if the spaceness of the social relations, that is, the spatial organization of which the region forms a part, is fully understood.

Just as the political economy framework explains regions in terms of the social relations of production, interaction between regions is also seen as a manifestation of productive relations. As Panagis Liossatos points out in chapter 5, this view contrasts sharply with the regional scientist's explanation of economic interaction between regions, which is based on trade or exchange relationships.

This difference holds important implications for explaining uneven regional development. Strict neoclassical trade analysis cannot explain how exchange of equal values in a competitive interregional (or international) marketplace gives rise to unequal regional development. Answers to that paradox have laid the blame on unequal terms of trade between regions, based on regional specialization in primary versus manufactured goods (Prebisch 1950), or on discrepancies between the value and price of goods, through which equal-valued goods may receive unequal prices in the interregional marketplace (Benetti 1974).

Liossatos argues, in the political economy framework, that uneven regional development "amounts to unequal relations between regionally based class fractions of capital." Moreover, uneven regional development can be perfectly consistent with the exchange of equal-valued commodities. Interregional transfers of surplus value, which are associated with uneven regional development, reflect discrepancies in regional capital intensities under conditions of full competition. The capital intensity, in turn, may reflect a different state of development of the forces of production and a different level of organization of the fraction of the working class the regional capitalists are confronted with. As a result, a fraction of capital in one region may receive a smaller share of the national income than it contributes.

It follows from political economy analysis of interregional relations that uneven regional development may accompany capitalist development but is not a necessary part of capitalist development. There may be greater inequality between class fractions of capital within a region than between regions, or no inequality at all. What is important, then, is to detect the dominant technical and social relations of production, determining the unequal relationships between fractions of capital. The spaceness of these relations — which may be largely international, as is true today — need not coincide with the spatial differentiation between territorially defined regions.

Applications of Regional Political Economy

The remaining chapters illustrate this key contribution of regional political economy — how the social relations that determine the spatial organization of a region may transcend the territorial limits of the region. Since the sixteenth century, social relations have been increasingly determined by the international division of labor: first under the mercantilist influence of Spanish colonialism, then under English-dominated industrial capitalism, and finally under U.S.-centered monopoly capitalism. The spatial organization of production — including, as we defined earlier, the relations of production — in particular regions and countries has reflected the changing international division of labor.

The most recent change became noticeable around 1970. This new international division of labor – called by some "the new international economic order" – has been at the root of such diverse changes in regional economics as the sunbelt boom in the United States and the transformation of peasant economies in developing countries. Because of the important historical and structural components in political economy analysis, regional political economists have been able to make this link between international division of labor and spatial organization and to discern recent changes in the international division of labor and their spatial impacts. The dialectical aspects of the methodology, however – treated as Coraggio counsels in chapter 3 – prevent the analysis from being unidirectional and overdeterministic.

Chapter 6, by Patricia Wilson Salinas, provides a clear application of regional political economy to a particular case that is especially useful for the reader who is unfamiliar with the political economy approach to regional analysis. It directly applies the major concepts of regional political economy, reviewed here, to analyzing the changing spatial organization in Peru. By starting with precolonial spatial organization and tracing the changes down to the current period, this analysis exemplifies one of the unique contributions of regional political economy – historical analysis that transcends one mode of production. Thus, the contrast with neoclassical regional science, which seeks to capture empirical regularities in spatial behavior within the framework of the capitalist mode of production only, is particularly sharp in this chapter.

This multimodal analysis also points out a major contribution of regional political economy to the study of developing countries. Most developing capitalist countries contain some regions in which precapitalist (that is, nonwage) relations of production predominate. These so-called backward regions, Salinas points out, are not underdeveloped, because modernization (that is, the capitalist mode of production) has not reached them. Rather, international capitalist development has incorporated these regions into a dependent role that takes advantage of (and maintains to a great degree) their precapitalist relations by creating mechanisms for transferring surplus from the underdeveloped to the developed capitalist regions. Thus, it is not the lack of capitalist development but the type of capitalist development – specifically, the international capitalist division of labor – that can perpetuate pockets of underdevelopment in developing countries.

Chapter 7, by David Barkin, uncovers a newer strategy – based on the new international division of labor – for profitably incorporating developing countries and their poorer regions into the world capitalist system. Maintaining precapitalist relations of production in regions of traditional peasant agriculture in order to appropriate a surplus from them in the form of cheap basic foodstuffs (which brings down the price of urban labor) and cheap seasonal labor provides only a limited amount of surplus for international capital.

Another strategy is to displace peasant agriculture with modern agriculture, producing for the international market according to national (and regional) comparative advantages. The development of export-oriented agriculture in developing countries provides a new opportunity for direct foreign investment in primary sector production, related industrial production (agro-industry), and international marketing of agricultural products, as well as increased demand for international agricultural inputs (equipment, seeds, technology, and so forth). This international strategy for agriculture reflects the new international division of labor – the integration of peripheral economies into the world capitalist market through the development of new exports based on comparative advantages. The strategy is being implemented primarily in the most advanced developing countries, particularly those that have a cooperative national government.

In Mexico, where public policy has facilitated implementation of the internationalization strategy, relations of production in the agricultural regions have been changing rapidly. Barkin traces these impacts in terms of changes in (1) technology and product mix, (2) the agricultural work process and decisionmaking, (3) vulnerability to international forces, and (4) agro-industrialization. Barkin makes a clear case that the changing spatial organization of agriculture in Mexico can be understood only in the international context.

Chapter 8, by Thierry Noyelle, examines a different aspect of the new international division of labor and traces its impacts on urban and regional development in an advanced country, the United States. Whereas Barkin discusses the gradual incorporation of more regions into production for the international market, Noyelle examines the restructuring of industry on an international scale. In response to increasing competition in world markets, multinational corporations are reorganizing the process of production on a world scale, in terms of what is produced, how it is produced, and where it is produced. Multinational firms are adding a vast array of producer services to make their products more competitive; they are introducing more labor-saving technology and lowering skill requirements of the work process in order to use cheaper labor; and they are redeploying their capital geographically to obtain access to the cheaper labor and to reorganize the division of labor among their production facilities for a single global market rather than for a series of national markets (for example, the "world" car). Noyelle traces the impacts of these processes on spatial organization, or the spaceness of social relations, in the United States.

One of Noyelle's major contributions is to provide a historical, structural explanation of the sunbelt boom and frostbelt decline. Many regional analysts have treated the issue, usually in terms of regional factor price equilibrium or changing comparative regional advantages. These explanations have discussed the transfer of investment from one region to another and the changing sectoral composition of that investment in each region. Using regional political economy analysis, however, Noyelle is able to link these changes to the new international division of labor and the accompanying trend of industrial restructuring, on the one hand, and to important related domestic changes, on the other hand – namely, the demise of the neo-Keynesian era, the breakup of the alliance between big capital and big labor, and the passing of the consumer society.

Specifically, Noyelle traces the spatial impact of these changes well beyond the simplistic sunbelt-frostbelt dichotomy and, based on a three-tiered classification system of U.S. cities, finds a changing urban hierarchy in which a minority of cities is benefitting – that is, those with high concentrations of employment in corporate offices, producer services, and public sector services. In these top-tier service centers, a bifurcated labor market is likely to develop in which the growth of high-level primary sector jobs and low-level secondary sector jobs outpaces the growth of intermediate-level jobs (known as subordinate primary jobs). In the growing number of lower-tiered specialized production centers characterized by the importance of consumer services, retailing, or the assembly industry, secondary jobs are likely to predominate. In both cases the intermediate-level jobs – "the major channel of upward mobility for labor and the fruits of the earlier big labor-big business alliance – are likely to be disappearing."

Chapter 9, by Robert Cohen, exemplifies Noyelle's analysis of industrial restructuring for a specific industry – the automobile industry. Analyzing the European and American automobile industries, Cohen finds that greater competition in the world market has, indeed, triggered corporate strategies to integrate production globally rather than nationally or regionally. He traces those strategies in detail, emphasizing implications for the spatial reorganization of production. While utilizing some elements of neoclassical location theory, Cohen's discussion highlights the contribution of regional political economy in explaining the roots of major shifts in locational decision criteria.

In Chapter 10, Frank Moulaert continues on the theme of industrial restructuring and growing duality in the labor market, this time applied strictly to the European situation. In tracing the implications of the restructuring on Belgium, he finds that, although part of the corporate restructuring strategy is gradual bifurcation of the labor market into high-skilled and low-skilled jobs, the geographic strategy followed by large corporations differs from that in the United States. Rather than redirecting investments toward regions of cheaper or more compliant labor, corporations use the public sector to bring cheaper labor directly to the traditional producing region, through a migration policy that stimulates and checks labor migration from southern Europe according to the needs of capital.

This final chapter illustrates well another major contribution of regional political economy — analyzing the role of the State (or the public sector) with respect to the relations of production and their spaceness. Although it is discussed theoretically in chapter 4 and included to some extent in most of the chapters dealing with applications, the analysis of the role of the State is applied in greatest detail in chapter 10. The theory of the State in political economy views the State as an arena in which the conflicts between social classes and their fractions can be played out, although, in practice, the State usually is responsive to the needs of large capital. Moulaert documents that such is the case with Belgian immigration policy. He concludes that labor unions, which have been struggling to get jobs upgraded by reducing the flow of immigrant labor, should focus their efforts not only on the State but also on direct negotiations with capital around the organization of production and the work process.

In sum, the major implication of this book is that spatial analysis is or should be much more than a highly specialized examination of one aspect of societal structure. Rather, spatial analysts must grasp the total logic of the development of the productive system and its social relations, must see related developments on the level of the superstructure of laws and plans and ideologies, and must explain spatial organization as a manifestation of these developments. In the current period of international capitalism, that determining logic is bound up in the changing international division of labor.

Notes

1. There are several good introductory and comprehensive textbooks on regional science (Isard 1956; Isard and Smith 1969; Richardson 1969; and Paelinck and Nijkamp 1975).

2. For a review of this literature, see Edel et al. (1978).

3. These concepts are derived from Marxian political economy. See Marx (1859, 1967). *Contribution to the Critique of Political Economy* (various editions, 1859) and *Capital,* three volumes (New York: International Publishers, 1967; originally published in 1861).

4. There is one exception. When the forces of production are developed to a level that obviates scarcity, the objective conditions for the emergence of a society free of such struggle are there.

References

Benetti, C. 1974. *Valeur et Repartition.* Paris: Maspero.

Edel, Candace Kim; Edel, Mathew; Fox, Kenneth; Markusen Ann; Meyer, Peter; and Varl, David. 1978. "Uneven Regional Development: An Introduction to this Issue." *Review of Radical Political Economics,* Special Issue on Uneven Regional Development, 10:1-12.

Isard, Walter. 1956. *Location and Space Economy.* Cambridge, Mass.: MIT Press.

Isard, Walter, and Smith, T. 1969. *General Theory, Social, Political, Economic, and Regional.* Cambridge, Mass.: MIT Press.

Marx, Karl. 1859. *Contributions to the Critique of Political Economy* (various editions).

______. 1967. *Capital,* 3 vols. New York: International Publishers (originally published in 1861).

Paelinck, Jean, and Nijkamp, Peter. 1975. *Operational Theory and Method in Regional Economics.* Westmead, England: Saxon House.

Prebisch, Raul. 1950. *The Economic Development of Latin America and Its Principal Problems.* New York: United Nations.

Richardson, Harry. 1969. *Regional Economics.* New York: Praeger.

I THEORY, METHODS, AND CONCEPTS

2 THE THEORIES AND METHODS OF REGIONAL SCIENCE AND REGIONAL POLITICAL ECONOMY COMPARED

Frank Moulaert

Neoclassical regional science integrates space into the analysis of social reality in two basic ways. First, space comes in as distance — as the physical separation of economic decision makers and of markets. To bring economic decision makers into communication with one another, to combine factors of production into a process of production at the same location, or to make finished commodities available at markets that are far from the point of production, distance must be bridged. Therefore, along with other inputs, transportation inputs are needed in the process of production; and transportation becomes a commodity that consumers are willing to have, or must have, in their commodity bundle. Second, all economic agents and activities use land — that is, physical space. Any production unit needs land as an input, and any consumption unit, or household, needs land to "hold its house" on. In sum, orthodox regional science deals with space in the form of transportation problems and land use problems.

Regional science has substantially enriched neoclassical economic theory, which regards transportation problems and land use problems as marginal to the overall economic issue. Regional science helps in understanding how different economic activities are located in different or similar locations; how linked economic activities are spread or concentrated in space; how regions show a locational pattern that follows an economic rationale; and how urban areas are complementary to surrounding rural areas. Thus, regional science has applied the orthodox model of rational economic behavior either to understanding the existing physical organization of space or to prescribing an optimal organization of space — as in the literature on optimal regionalization and city size.

Regional science has gone even further. It has introduced the problem of conflicts between regions and the problem of the political organization of regions and systems of regions; it has devoted considerable attention to environmental problems; it has stressed the importance of multidisciplinary approaches; and, very recently, it has shown openness to the political and economic aspects of federalism and regionalism. Regional science has made such impressive contributions to the study of social reality in its "spaceness" that the question immediately arises of what a political economy approach to the regional issue could add to the understanding of the "spaceness" of social reality.

In fact, the goal of the political economist dealing with a regional problem is not to add to the analysis of neoclassical regional scientists. This is impossible, for two closely related reasons. First, the regional political economist starts from a general view of social reality that rests on the Marxian insights into the working of capitalism; this is in complete disaccord with the neoclassical world view adopted by most regional scientists. Second, the methodology of a political economist is completely different from that of the orthodox regional scientist. Whereas the political economist adopts historical dialectics as his or her methodology, the regional scientist remains, like the neoclassical economic theoretician, a true believer in positivism. This difference in methodology, together with the difference in view, leads to very different conclusions on how the social system works.

The difference between regional science and regional political economy is rooted in the antagonistic content of the economic schools from which they originate. Therefore, an understanding of what is special about regional political economy requires an understanding of what is special about political economy. The following section elaborates on the difference in methodology and world view between the two schools.[1]

Dialectical Materialism

The political economy approach to social reality has a dialectical and a historical aspect that are inseparably related to each other. *Dialectical* refers to the Marxian way of reasoning, which starts from the philosophical belief that, as Heilbroner (1980) puts it, "the innermost nature of things [is] *dynamic* and *conflictual,* rather than inert and static." To understand the dynamics of reality, it is necessary to know the relationships that give the tangible elements of reality their meaning. Thus, people only have a meaning through the social relations that exist between them. Moreover, upon distinguishing the relations between people, it becomes clear that the label *people* is no more than a black box or, according to Marx, a "chaos"; it is certainly not a useful category for social analysis. Therefore, to be useful to social analysis, people must be looked upon according to their different moments, determined by the social relations to which they belong – for example, capitalists and workers in the social relations of production; producers and consumers in the social relations of exchange.

Three principles underly the political economy theory of social relations. First, the study of relations (versus tangible elements) requires that social reality be viewed as a unity or, to use a more operational concept, as a structure. Relations form a whole; they are the constituent elements of the structure but, at the same time, they are themselves determined by the structure to which they belong.

Second, the relations are of an intrinsically dynamic nature; that is, they are susceptible to change, not only because they form part of a unity with other changing relations but because they can be *conflictual* (such as the relations between classes) or *contradictory.* A good example of the latter dynamics in the capitalist mode of production is the contradiction between the need of capital to maximize the appropriateness of surplus labor, and the need for sufficient markets in which to turn products into profit. The first need requires low wages and a substantial unemployed or subemployed labor reserve, which decreases the purchasing power of the working class and thus is contradictory to the second need, that of ensuring sufficient demand. In short, part of the dynamics of social relations results from the contradictions and conflicts that are present in social reality. The analysis of these contradictions and conflicts within a dynamic societal structure is known as dialectical analysis.

The third principle is that social relations can be understood only in their historical context. The interpretation of history used by political economists is Marxian-based materialism. The materialist interpretation of history concludes that the mode of production (that is, the way in which activities that provide the primary needs of humankind are socially organized) conditions the social, political, and intellectual life in history. The mode of production is the unifying principle of social relations and enables the analyst to define structures of social reality.

Economic Idealistic Positivism

As dialectical materialism is the basis of both the methodology and the view of social reality shared by political economists, the methodology and view shared by neoclassical economists is economic idealistic positivism. *Positivism* is a general term for contemporary scientific methods that accept relations between the elements of reality only if they can be tested – that is, if empirical evidence exists supporting the acceptance of the assumed relation or the rejection of an antagonistic relation.

There are several immediate consequences of the application of positivist methods for scientific inquiry into social reality. First, only measurable attributes of elements and relations are eligible for analysis. A corollary of this first consequence is that the elements considered in the analysis are atomistic – that is, they are easily discernible from another entity (for example, one consumer, with a budget, faced with a set of priced commodities). This implies that, because of their structural character, more abstract relational elements, such as classes, are excluded from positivist analysis. It also means that the structural aspects of discernible elements are excluded from the analysis. Second, given the available testing procedures, the statics of a relation are studied primarily; that is, the qualitative dynamics of relations falls beyond the scope of positivist inquiry. A third consequence of the positivist approach is that, since it does not include the study of the qualitative dynamics of relations, it cannot possibly deal with interrelational dynamics in the way dialectics does. In sum, the main contrast between dialectics and positivism is that dialectics deals with the dynamics of relations and elements within a dynamic structure, whereas positivism restricts itself to the measurable aspects of relations between tangible, discernible elements.

Given the foregoing distinctions between positivism and dialectics, what about idealism versus materialism? The term *idealistic* refers to the neoclassical view of man and society. It is, in essence, the view of nineteenth-century liberal thinkers who regarded the human being as a free being who lived to fulfill his personal aspirations; moreover, they believed that, if every person sought to satisfy his own needs in a rational way – that is, in an attempt to maximize his satisfaction – this would also produce his best contribution to the creation of a prosperous and harmonious world. In this way, a view of an ideal world filled the minds of many liberal thinkers of that century. It also inspired the minds of generations of neoclassical economists, who developed the model of the free-choosing rational consumer seeking to maximize his utility level; of the energetic and strictly rational producer, ever combining the available quantities of factors of production in an optimal way so as to maximize revenues or profits; of the society of free and rationally optimizing consumers and producers that, through the intervention of a price system, manages to let wealth grow in social harmony. Obviously, that model is a persiflage of the world as viewed by political economists. The harmony and voluntaristic action that characterize the neoclassical model are in sharp contrast with the world of contradiction, domination, and struggle detected by the political economist. It is also apparent why neoclassical economics does not pay much attention to historical or structural analysis. If one were to ask for the neoclassical view of the role of history, the likely answer would be that, for neoclassical economists, changes in society are so gradual or so predictable from the behavioral models of the rational economic agents and society that dynamic historical analysis becomes superfluous.

Conclusion

This comparison of the methodologies and world views of political economists and neoclassical economists makes it clear that the differences are so fundamental that it is correct to argue, as I did at the beginning of this chapter, that political economy does not add to the analysis by neoclassical economists but, instead, offers a completely different analysis. The difference is not, as is often argued, that regional political economy covers more subjects of a political nature (such as the role of the state, regionalism, unionization), because neoclassical economists also cover many political subjects. The difference is that the issue related to these subjects is defined and analyzed in a completely different way because of the very different theory and methodology used. The following chapters illustrate these differences.

Notes

1. The following exploration of political economy is based primarily on three sources (Heilbroner 1980; Harnecker 1974; de Janvry and Garramon 1977).

References

Freyssenet, M. 1977. *La Division Capitaliste du Travail.* Paris: Savelli.

Harnecker, Martha. 1974. *Les Concepts Elementaires du Materialisme Historique.* Brussels: Editions Contradictions.

Heilbroner, Robert. 1980. *Marxism: For and Against.* New York: Norton & Company.

de Janvry, Alain, and Garramon, Carlos. 1977. "Laws of Motion of Capital in the Center-Periphery Structure." *The Review of Radical Political Economics,* pp. 29-38.

Moulaert, Frank. 1979–1980. "On the Nature and Scope of Complex Conflicts." *Papers (Peace Science Society International),* Vol. 9, 2, pp. 48-66.

3 SOCIAL SPACENESS AND THE CONCEPT OF REGION

Jose Luis Coraggio

This chapter sets forth the conceptual foundations that differentiate regional political economy from current idealistic approaches to spatial analysis. To do so requires a thorough criticism of dominant regional theories on three interwoven grounds: philosophical, theoretical, and methodological. New ontological demarcations, theoretical concepts, and methods are required. This is not simply a matter of changing a few assumptions or adding variables to the existing models. Rather, this chapter attempts to build a new *topica*. At the end of the chapter, the implications of the theoretical conclusions for the concrete analysis of the regional problem in Latin America are illustrated.

The physicalist approach that prevails in regional science confuses physical with social laws. This confusion cannot be avoided by merely modernizing the underlying physical theory or replacing it with a biological one. Methodologically, the physicalist approach goes hand in hand with the use and abuse of analogy as a means of producing knowledge. The political economy approach, in contrast, is based on materialism, which relies not on isomorphisms but rather on the direct determination of social phenomena. Regional political economy depends on a categorical analysis of space, which sets a proper ontological foundation for the concept of region.[1]

Having concluded that the understanding of social spaceness requires a previous understanding of social processes, the question then arises *which* social theory is appropriate for such a purpose. The materialist approach of po-

---

An expanded treatment of this subject can be found in Jose Luis Corragio and David Barkin, eds., *La Cuestion Regional en America Latina* (Mexico: El Colegio de Mexico, 1982).

litical economy rejects neoclassical economic theory and method and adopts Marxian social theory, which centers on the production and reproduction of social relations.

Categorical Analysis

The categorical analysis of an existing real complex involves (1) discriminating between its different modalities of being (for example, a commodity is a physical object, corporeal in extent and time, with various use qualities, but it is also a social object, an exchange value); (2) identifying the categories pertaining to each modality; and (3) establishing the articulation between the different categories.[2]

Except in less-developed forms of being, we do not encounter real formations (systems of concrete relations) that are purely representative of one stratum of being. Thus, a society is made up not of a category system that pertains exclusively to the social order but rather of a category system that is intermingled with categories that pertain to the natural order, without which the social whole could not exist effectively. Hence, one sees the importance of clarifying the relationship between nature and society for social analysis. The categories of natural order, however, which are present in formations of a higher order, undergo a variation from one stratum to another. As such, in a theoretical social topica, one cannot establish the nature-society relationship as an interaction between two entities, since society has natural conditions pertaining to its modality of being, which operate within it as determinations of existence.

This does not imply that all categories of the natural strata become categories of social being. One must establish the difference between constitutive determinations of a field and factors present in it. When we say that a determination is constitutive, we mean that its exclusion impedes our comprehension of the phenomenon in its essential nature. Thus, excluding social relations of production from the analysis of a society would impede our understanding of its dynamics. However, to grasp these dynamics, we might well overlook the empirically undeniable fact that capitalists are congenital bipeds. It is thus necessary to discriminate between categories and other determinations that are not fundamental, so that we do not fall into analyticism without guide and without end.

The Category of Space

Analysis of the category *space* has been based fundamentally on problems pertaining to physics and mathematics. In the social sciences, the term *space* is used loosely by simply adding the adjective *social, economic,* or *political.* In many cases, the resulting term merely denotes certain territorial divisions of economic, political, or other significance. Thus, practically no difference is made between space and region. Moreover, the social determination, which would establish a difference with respect to the natural one, usually appears as a simple alternative and parallel criterion to divide segments of territory (natural regions as opposed to economic regions, and the like). The correct procedure for a rigorous study would be to start with an analysis of the category of space in relation to natural processes and then to establish the way in which this category enters into social processes through the relationship between nature and society.

Real space is a category, a constitutive determination of physical objects, in which the term *object* is not limited to things but also designates relations and processes. One cannot devise theoretical systems that account for physical processes without a conceptualization of the spaceness of the phenomena. Space is not something that is alongside other physical objects; rather, it is their condition of existence. According to idealistic conceptions, things occupy or leave empty space. If this were the case, spatial form, or the relations of position or movement, also could exist outside space and eventually could be introduced into it. This impossibility of existence without the spatial substratum is the point of our statement that space is a constitutive and inseparable determination of physical things and processes, or that these things and processes are spatial. Regional political economists also reject conceptions that substantiate space. Space does not exist by itself. As is the case for time, its fundamental categorical moment is dimensionality. It is impossible, however, for the dimensions to exist beyond the thing of which they are the dimensions.

Spaceness in the Social Order

Space does not constitute a category of social order.[3] However, insofar as social relations and processes are realized only by means of entities that have a physical and biological substratum, any concrete social formation has a natural as well as a social nature. From this point of view, we may speak of the spaceness of social objects or processes as being indirect with regard to the social but direct with regard to the corresponding physical supports. Then, however, one should ask if social spaceness will not reduce itself to the physical spaceness of those supports. If the question is put in these terms, the answer is negative. However, physical spaceness is acting as the basis for social spaceness.

Social relations – for example, economic relations – link concrete agents of the social system. Those agents, insofar as they share a physical substratum, have a spaceness founded on moments of physical spaceness, such as relative position and direction of movement, whose logic, however, is social, not physical.[4] The buying and selling relation, for example, implies a material circulation of a commodity from the place where its owner-seller had it to the location of the buyer. In a competitive mercantile system, the territorial configuration of the places of production, storage, and marketing, and the intervening paths traveled, are explained not on the basis of physical laws but on the laws of circulation under competitive mercantilism. If other social determinations are added to this, the spaceness of the commodity could be modified. If juridical relations establish that certain commodities cannot leave the country, for example, although the laws of the market would make the ambits of circulation go beyond the frontiers, we have a spaceness determined not only in economic but also in juridical-political terms.

Spaceness is not space; neither is it a spatial configuration nor an actual spatial form. It refers, rather, to the possible spatial configurations, and often to the most probable ones. If we speak of organization, however, not merely of configuration, we are thinking in terms of recurrence, processes, relative stability, and structures. The explanation of a relative location or a movement cannot be reduced to the reconstruction of a chain of cause-and-effect connections (of whatever order) resulting in that location or movement. Many concrete movements and locations may well be considered fortuitous for a social explanation, although they may be traced step by step to form a specific sequence of a particular process of another order. The concrete must be conceived as a synthesis of multiple determinations of various orders, understanding by synthesis not their mere addition but their structured articulation.

Therefore, regional political economists do not reduce social spaceness to physical spaceness, as the physicalists do; neither do they claim that social spaceness is purely social – that is, without natural determinations. Rather, the spaceness of social phenomena is indirect, based on the articulation between nature and society, but with social laws more determinant than natural laws. Likewise, social spaceness is historically determined and has no universal character.

Spatial Configuration and Spatial Organization

Thus far, we have clarified that the spaceness of social phenomena is indirect – that is, derived from the fact that social relations require physical supports. It is obvious, then, that the concepts of spatial form and configuration refer to those supports and that their sense will be deduced from the knowledge of the laws that govern the corresponding social phenomena.

To build up the concept of spatial organization, we shall start from the concept of spatial configuration. A spatial configuration is the particular distribution of a set of physical objects, projected onto a continuous surface or onto a network of nodes and arcs. For objects that are not in any fixed manner localized with respect to the surface or network of reference, the concept of configuration is extended to the paths described by their movement. When the projection is made onto the concrete surface of the earth, we use the term *territorial configuration*. By *territory* or *territorial surface,* we refer to the usual geographical concept, including its mineral elements, soils, flora and fauna, climate, and topography.

When a spatial (territorial) configuration is supported by a social process that strengthens and preserves it, or when it is the product of voluntary acts toward certain conscious aims, we shall call it *spatial (territorial) organization*. Spatial organization refers to those spatial configurations that are mediated by social processes. By *process* we do not mean *any* sequence of events but a sequence that constitutes a recurring cycle. Process implies repetition, self-regulation, permanency of conditions for a cyclical movement, and, therefore, structure and the possibility of reproduction of that structure, at least while the process lasts.[5]

However, any historical sequence of events does not constitute a scientific explanation insofar as one cannot deduce the determinisms that properly connect such events. By *historical process,* we do not mean every sequence that necessarily takes place in time but a historically determined process (non-universal, noneternal). For instance, the sequence of events resulting in an increasing agglomeration of people and activities in a given city can be understood only in the context of a historically determined system of social relations. If we remain at the level of appearances, we can simply state that the agglomeration attracts people from other parts, just as greater masses attract smaller ones, and we shall be content with a physicalistic pseudo-explanation of the observed phenomenon. Following this reasoning, it would be difficult to arrive at the hypothesis that, in a given stage of the capitalist system, there is a tendency for the labor force to concentrate in big cities as a general condition for individual capitalist accumulation; neither one would foresee that, in other stages of capitalist development, such a tendency could start to reverse.

Before proceeding, we shall propose a gradation in terminology, differentiating between *configuration* and *organization* on one side and *form* on the other side. The first term alludes to any distribution, be it casual or legal, regular or irregular, expressible in terms of abstract formal systems or only in terms of itself (as in a photograph). The term *organization* is more specific in that it requires the existence of a social process to which the configuration is associated. We propose to reserve the term *spatial form* for those distributions that have (1) a logic derivable from some social process and (2) identifiable regularity and recurrence.

The Relationship Between Spatial Forms and Social Processes

It is not easy to uncover the determining relations between social processes and spatial forms. With respect to the different orders of determination, we propose that it is impossible to give one sole and general answer that is applicable to all historical situations. The relationship between the social categories and the natural ones is not unequivocally established for any form of society. The possibility of setting up laws determining relationships between structures, processes, or social relations, on the one hand, and spatial forms, on the other, is closely linked to the possibility of clarifying the articulated scheme of determinisms of different orders and types that link the social processes to particular spatial organizations that are differentiable and recurring (that is, spatial forms).

As a schematic example, let us take the case of the territorial organization of population in the form of urban agglomerations in a capitalist system. The growing relative agglomeration is a change in the territorial configuration of the population, which we postulate to respond to a social migration process. This process contains several determinisms, of different types.[6] It has a statistical determinism, in the sense that its law can be expressed probabilistically in its general features and for relatively short periods. However, if we assume that this level is the only level of explanation (as, for example, when Markov chains are posed as a theory of migration), we would be far from comprehending the phenomenon in its real nature.

The social migration process also contains a teleological determinism, in the sense that individuals can make migration decisions independent of an explicit, formal, means-end analysis. However, if we were to attribute migration exclusively to individual attitudes (as, for example, when the analysis of migrations is based on methods of surveying and identifying individual independent factors), we would not be able to understand migration as part of a social process. Behavior, or individual attitudes, when faced with certain conditions, cannot be seen as innate or natural to the human being; rather, it is seen as the product of a historical totality to which the migrating individuals belong. The social system as a whole, then, is at the genesis of the determination, as a structural determinism. Thus, workers who, for their reproduction, have only the wages they receive from selling their labor power, will have a migratory behavior that in no way can be thought of as innate to the human being.[7]

Moreover, the concrete configurations that the migratory flows adopt do not stem from those behaviors fulfilling themselves in a vacuum but are conditioned by other processes in which functional determinisms or determinisms of reciprocal causation operate. This is the case, for example, when the development of the productive forces of industry requires a transformation of the forms of production in certain agricultural regions. These processes, which are constitutive of the process of social capital reproduction, are typical of a social structure dominated by the capitalist mode of production. However, this mode of production is formed internally by a dialectical determinism derived from its contradictory nature. If we do not understand this contradictory nature, it will be impossible to comprehend the social, and therefore the historical, dynamics of the capitalist mode of production.[8]

If we were to try to reduce determinism to one type, even one of a high order, such as structural determinism, we could not construct a scientific explanation of the phenomenon under investigation. Rather, the mutual articulation and the concrete ways of realization of the different types of determinisms involved must be understood. For example, structural determinism operates through concrete institutions and social agents. To try to establish propositions on the relationship between the mode of production and spatial organization will be a speculative exercise if it is not supported by an analytical, empirically based approach, which interweaves the different determinisms that mediate between both terms of the relationship. Thus, with regard to the question of the relationship between social processes and spatial forms, there is no general answer that covers all historical situations. In each case, it is necessary to establish the types and orders of determinism that are relevant.

The Concept of Region as Spatial Organization

To define region in political economy terms, one more concept must be introduced: the concept of territorial ambit of a relationship. The territorial ambit of a particular social relation is the segment of territory that includes the (transformed) location of agents and means directly coupled by the relation, as well as the pathways of the material flows that realize it. It is also possible to determine areas corresponding to relatively homogeneous relationships between agents and elements, or to be certain of their attributes – for example, areas of peasant agricultural production, areas occupied by certain ethnic groups, areas that contain families with similar annual incomes, and areas with the same principal output. Territorial ambits of relationships and territorial areas that are homogeneous in this manner are called *regions.*

Perhaps as a reaction against geographical currents that emphasize what is territorial *per se,* some authors have applied the term *region* to social subsystems, even speaking of *regional socioeconomic formations* as a term that could replace the term *region*. We believe that, just as one should not confuse a national society with its territory, one should not confuse a social subsystem with its corresponding region. The concept of region that we use refers, then, to segments of territory as locus, be they subnational or supernational, and not to the relations of which they are the ambits, the agents located in them, the flows they include, or the natural elements they contain. The region does not exist beyond and independently of the relations and elements located in it, but neither does it coincide with them.[9]

Although, as a locus, the region has no content in itself, as a segment of concrete territory, it has its own content, given by its soil, topography, climate, mineral resources and so on. Hence, we must establish the relations that take place between this material region and the processes of the society located in it. Although we consider the social and the natural as different orders of being, when we refer to concrete social formations, we consider the natural as something not below the social but, rather, as something inside social structures and processes. We see the collectivity settled within a given region as a socio-natural complex. We reject the concept of region as (1) a spatial form plus natural content or (2) a spatial form plus natural content plus social content. The natural configuration is a factor that, within the given social processes, orients the concrete territorial configuration (and, eventually, the regionalization) of social phenomena but in no way produces it. Thus, natural determinism is already incorporated in the regulation of social processes – as, for example, in the material conditions for social reproduction – and is not added from outside. Whereas a region is a spatial form of a given social subset of agents, means, and relationships, regionalization (that is, the realization of relations under the form of different subsystems with their corresponding territorial ambits) is a spatial form of the whole society.

Social Processes and Regionalization

A region becomes relevant on the basis of the social process being studied. The social division of labor in the capitalist system, for example, has a spatial organization (which we call the territorial division of labor) that indicates one period of regionalization that constitutes a spatial form of advanced social production. The process of capital accumulation is also regionalized insofar as it is organized as a net of interwoven partial accumulation processes that have defined territorial ambits. Similarly, the social process of reproducing the labor force has a logic that relates, though not always directly, the regionalization of labor markets to the spatial organization of population. Moreover, the political and ideological processes of domination used to maintain the social relations of production have a spatial organization insofar as they evidence particular territorial ambits. Because these social processes are dynamic, their regionalization is also subject to reorganization.

Can this complex territorial organization and reorganization that accompany capitalist development be reduced to a simple law, such as the linear tendency of widening markets and extending capitalist relations, called by some the "tendency toward monopolistic homogenization of the economic space"?[10] On the contrary, this territorial reorganization will hardly be unidirectional and uniform for all the processes of social production. It is expected to be a contradictory process, the contradictions being expressed in terms of the ambits of the different relationships. For example, the ambits of exploitation and accumulation of one fraction of the bourgeoisie located in a certain place, maintained on the basis of local repressive mechanisms, may start to weaken if they enter into contradiction with the ambits of national and international capital in its process of expansion.

How will these contradictions be resolved, and how will regional ambits be redefined? It is difficult to predict this on the basis of a law of a global tendency toward homogenization. Rather, the regionalization of all those social processes that contribute to the reproduction of social relations must be studied — that is, those that reproduce the productive base as well as the social, political, and ideological superstructure. In national systems with incomplete development, for which the conditions of reproduction in many cases rest on external processes, the analysis of regionalization cannot be made without considering the different modalities of insertion into the world system.

The Regional Question in Latin America

The regional question in Latin America involves, first, the contradictory spatial organization resulting from the territorial organization and reorganization of the social processes dominated by capitalist relations. These processes of social reproduction may involve relations with other systems of production and domination, whose territorial ambits contradict the requirements of capitalist development. Second, the regional question in Latin America also involves unequal development of the productive forces, especially in regions that are peripheral to the process of capitalist accumulation but are exposed to violent modification because of the requirements imposed by the capitalist system. Third, it involves the appropriation of land or its insertion into the capitalist process of accumulation. Fourth, the regional question in Latin America involves the territorial ambits of politico-ideological domination and, therefore, the regionalization of social struggles.

Whether the issue is spatial organization or domination, the regional question is, without doubt, a social question. As such, we must approach it by leaving aside the schemes that reify space. Rather, we must look for the meaning of territorial organization by means of a scientific theory that accounts for the historical development of our countries without making jumps into the void. We must examine analytically the complex and never unequivocal interweaving of determinisms that concretely link social structures to spatial organization.

Notes

1. A first attempt at this analysis was presented in Coraggio (1979). It was attempted there to demonstrate, among other points (1) the impossibility of a theory of space in general and, consequently, (2) the need to reject the hypothesis that geometry could become a science of space, (3) the need to reject the hypotheses that physical spaceness (gravitation, and the like) is directly applicable to social phenomena, and (4) the need to start from a theory of social processes in order to investigate social spaceness.

Although regional political economists apparently accept the possibility that a scientific discipline exists that makes space and region its object of study, we are ready to admit, as soon as our research confirms it, that it might not be necessary to build up an alternative theory of space and region. We might very well conclude that there are no scientific grounds for such a theory and even less for a so-called regional science separate from the social sciences.

2. We are excluding the term *category* as a fundamental concept of a field of knowledge. Category as determination of existence is one thing, but the concept developed with respect to a particular category in a theoretical system is another. This question may appear arbitrary, especially since, even in the field of Marxian analysis, the second interpretation seems to have predominated.

3. This affirmation implies that the structural laws of a society can be comprehended by ignoring social spaceness in its different forms. However, when it is a question of investigating particular relationships in a concrete society, incorporating spaceness may sometimes prove indispensable, and it would be a mistake to deny this need simply because space is not a social category in the sense mentioned previously. It would also be a mistake to claim that the category of space is the "forgotten dimension" and place it in a position of pivot for the system of social categories. See, for example, the works of Edward Soja (1978), who attempts to found a kind of geographical materialism.

4. See Hartmann (1960). It is important to note the restricted sense of spatial movement. When we speak of the social circulation of a commodity, the concept of movement thus expressed does not necessarily include a spatial movement (material circulation).

5. A process has a conscious subject when it is regulated from the perspective of a plan that posits objectives and provides instruments to implement its objectives. When, on the contrary, there is the aforementioned condition of recurrence but there is no one conscious subject directing the process, as in the global process of capitalist accumulation (which has sometimes been

presented metaphorically as if there were a subject called "the invisible hand"), we say that it is a process without a conscious subject. In either case, there is the possibility of setting up legal connections between the processes and the spatial (or territorial) configurations of their material supports. If there is no process in the sense described, the explanation of the territorial configurations cannot be referred to any system with relative stability and, therefore, can only refer to its process of genesis or to what certain authors call its genealogy. See Lipietz (1977).

6. On the question of types of determinism, we lean upon the work of Mario Bunge (1959). The term *order* refers to natural, social, and so on. The term *type* refers to the model of determination that gives the character of law to the established relation.

7. See de Gaudemar (1979).

8. With this example, we have merely attempted to illustrate the question of the types of determinism. This way of putting it differs, for example, from the concept of pluricausality, which, in the case of migrations, would lead in the best of cases to speculation about the relative weight of personal and social causes of migrations.

9. For a different point of view, which in our opinion confuses levels of determination, see Sormani (1977).

10. See de Oliveira (1977). However, the analysis that de Oliveira makes in his first chapter offers the elements for organizing the analysis from a much more complex viewpoint. He proposes "a concept of region founded on the specificity of reproduction of capital, in the forms assumed by the accumulation process, the class structure peculiar to these forms and, therefore, also in the forms of class struggle and social conflict on a more general scale" (p. 27).

References

Bunge, Mario. 1959. *Causality: The Place of the Causal Principle in Modern Science.* Cambridge, Mass.: Harvard University Press.

Coraggio, J.L. 1979. "On the Possibilities and Difficulties of Radical Spatial Analysis." In *Comparative Urbanization Studies.* Los Angeles: University of California, School of Architecture and Planning.

de Gaudemar, Jean-Paul. 1979. *Movilidad del trabajo y acumulación de capital.* Mexico City: Ediciones Era.

de Oliveira, Francisco. 1977. *Elegía para una Re(li)giao.* Paz y Terra, Sao Paulo.

Hartmann, N. 1960. *Ontología,* vol. 4. Mexico City: F.C.E.

Lipietz, Alain. 1977. *Le Capital et son Espace.* Paris: Maspero.

Soja, Edward. 1978. " 'Topian Marxism and Spatial Praxis: A Reconsideration of the Political Economy of Space." Paper presented at the annual meeting of the American Geographical Association, New Orleans, April.

Sormani, Horacio A. 1977. "Formación social y formación espacial: Hacia una dialéctica de los asentamientos humanos." *Estudios Sociales Centroamericanos,* no. 17.

4 REGIONS AND REGIONALISM

Ann R. Markusen

The concepts of region and regionalism have assumed an uneasy place in the political economy analysis of capitalist development. This chapter attempts to clarify the uses and misuses of the regional category for political economists. Presented first is an inquiry into the social relations that underlie regional concerns and an assertion that the notion of region cannot be given the same theoretical status held by class, gender, and certain cultural categories in the political economy lexicon but that it may be possible to posit abstractly a workable definition of regionalism. The following section explores the multiple roots of regional social relations that may form the basis for regionalism: economic relations from the structure of the mode of production, household material relations from the mode of reproduction of labor, and cultural social relations. Next, the special case of the State is covered, with an assertion that the State's own particular set of social relations plays a central role in regionalism. Building on these elements, a political economy definition of regionalism is proposed, using notions of territoriality, one or more of several possible sets of regional social relations, and political claims on some arm of the State. Following this is a reconsideration of the meaning of the region in political economy analysis, with an attempt to move from the definition of regionalism to that of region, concluding that regions exist and are meaningful for political economists only as empirical phenomena that must be subjected to concrete, historical, case-by-case analysis. Research in both regional political economy and regional science is taken to task for making fetishes of regions and for suggesting implicitly that regions are economic actors within a sort of social relations of place, in which one place exploits another. Finally, implications are drawn for ongoing research in regional political economy.

Regions and Regionalism as Social Relations

Regional political economists, who base their analysis largely on Marxian theory, find themselves on uncomfortable terrain. The concept of region is not a fundamental Marxian category. Nevertheless, entities called regions have been and are an important, sometimes primary, object of human struggle. For regional political economists, the significance of a region lies in the struggles over and within it, not in the entity *per se*. If regions were not the basis of or the arena for conflict, the study of them would be uninteresting and perhaps nonexistent. The purpose of a workable political economy definition of region, then, is to capture the causes of and grounds for such conflict. Such a definition must affirm the existence of the social relations of regions.

Unlike the definitions of State[1] and class, which refer unambiguously to social groups or hierarchies, the definition of region is problematic for political economists from the outset.[2] Region connotes a territorial, not social, entity.[3] The primacy of social relations in political economy analysis requires either that territorial units correspond one-on-one with social relations or that the use of region as a category of analysis be subordinated to categories of social relations. If the latter practice is required, then regions cannot be spoken of abstractly but always must be identified by the social relations that characterize them in a given instance. In other words, their concrete historical context must be given.

Both formally and informally, political economists have sometimes slipped into the use of region as an abstract conceptual category. The most explicit argument for the existence of spatial relations of production is given by Soja (1978). He implies that places have theoretically specifiable relations with one another. Less explicitly, regional political economists and their regional science counterparts frequently resort to language that characterizes regions as active agents in the development process. We might say, for example, that the southern region is experiencing uneven development or, worse, that the South is attracting jobs away from the North. Here the notions of region and job become substitutes for the economic actors – capital and labor – that Marxian theory specifies as the active agents in the development process. Throughout this chapter, an attempt will be made to show that regions cannot be unambiguously equated abstractly with any set of social relations. If so, regional political economists must develop a more innovative vocabulary for talking about the phenomenon of regional conflict in a theoretical way.

Two definitional possibilities exist. One is to eschew the noun *region* and to use only the adjective *regional* to qualify other categories. This subordinates the spatial to the social. If we say "regional development," for instance, we mean development in its concrete territorial form, not the development of regions themselves. The reification of space does not occur. Perhaps more useful, however, is the concept of regionalism – that is, the espousal of a territorial claim by some social group. Regionalism is a social phenomenon about which it may be possible to make some theoretical statements and endow with an abstract meaning. If regionalism turns out to be a complex social phenomenon, we may be able to specify the various forms it can take, drawn from empirical observations. In the following sections, the term *regionalism* will be employed rather than *region,* because it focuses more directly on the territorial social conflicts that are the concern of regional political economy. Although regionalism is clearly a subjective and experiential term, it may also refer to the objective social dynamics that cause territorial differences in social formations.

We can investigate the social relations that constitute regionalism by beginning with the Marxian notion of alienation. The notion of alienation compares the reality of human experience with an ideal in which the human community exists free of any institution or relation by which one group is denied full access to the fruits of their efforts or to the collective shaping of community culture. One form of alienation exists when a division of labor in material production develops whereby one group (designated a class) compels another group or class, through control over the means of production, to labor to support both groups. This particular division of labor and exploitation of one class by another constitutes the basis of political economy analysis of the mode of production.[4] Examples of modes are slavery in the classical era (slaves and slaveowners), feudalism in the Middle Ages (serfs and landlords), and capitalism in contemporary times (wage workers and capitalists). Marx investigated, in detail, the division of labor in the capitalist production of commodities, working out analytically the organization of the capitalist workplace, in which capitalists, who own the means of production and control the work process, exploit workers, who are forced to sell their labor power at a wage lower than the value of what they produce. Capitalist organization involves the appropriation of the product of labor from the worker and the worker's loss of both control over working conditions and the community guarantee of material security in childhood and old age.

In understanding regionalism, it is necessary to analyze the additional sets of institutions that, together with production, govern relationships within the human community: the household, the State, and the set of cultural institutions.[5] Each of these institutions has significant interrelationships with the capitalist workplace and its social relations but has an organization of the expenditure and appropriation of human labor time that differs from capitalist production relations. These may be the subject of struggle, regional or otherwise.

Any one of these institutions, if it involves oppression or exploitation, can lead to alienation from the human community.[6] For expository purposes, we will separate the institutions into two groups: those that concern the expenditure of human labor power directly in production and reproduction and those that encompass the political and cultural life of the community. Since each has its role in the analysis of regionalism, the next section will focus on each in turn, with the warning, however, that the interrelationships among these institutions frequently underlie the struggles over regionalism.

The Multiple Roots of Regional Social Relations

The Mode of Production

The organization of human society is fundamentally structured around one or more modes of production, which govern the social relations and techniques of production involved in the production of use values with human labor.[7] Not merely the mode of production itself but a number of features of its economic and social structure can serve as the basis for the evolution of regionalism. These features include the territorial incidence of class structure, the territorial pattern of production sectors, and the differential degrees of development of the productive forces across regions and of development of social relations of production across regions.

Specifying the mode or modes of production that characterize societies experiencing regionalism is clearly the appropriate starting point. For instance, an understanding of contemporary regionalism in the United States requires exploration of at least three modes of production: primitive communalism (Native Americans), slavery (the South prior to the Civil War), and capitalism (originally the North, and currently the entire economy). The first two modes did not exist in pure form but were shaped by capitalism in its ascendancy, at least insofar as they have figured in regional struggles. Capitalism, moreover, needs to be understood through several stages of its development: petty commodity production (a survival of the passage from feudalism to capitalism), primitive accumulation and mercantile capitalism, and industrial capitalism, now characterized as monopoly capitalism. Each stage has produced a different array of productive forces and social classes. The clash of people with positions in different modes may become a regional struggle, depending on the territorial placement of each. For instance, the Native American defense against European colonialism and the southern slaveholders' defense against northern industrial capitalism became regional struggles because of the spatial concentration of each protagonist group.

Even within a mode, such as capitalism, it is possible for classes to be unevenly distributed territorially, so that class conflicts take on a regional form. Working-class communities facing absentee mine owners, for instance, become class-based regional struggles (for example, South Africa, Appalachia). Similarly, differences in sectoral composition of production across territories may result in conflicts between needs of classes in different sectors. For instance, in the United States today, corporations in the energy sector in the West find their needs conflicting with the needs of the manufacturing sector in the East. Sometimes class and sectoral differences coincide. An example is the struggle between western family farmers and eastern capitalist interests (finance, railroads, steel, manufacturing in general) in the nineteenth-century United States.

Finally, spatial differentiation in the development of a mode of production may serve as the substance of a regional conflict. Differential development of the productive forces of capitalism, such as the level of sophistication of technology, may result in regional antagonisms between capitalist classes or coalitions of classes; or differential development of social relations, such as the territorial incidence of unionization or community organization for collective consumption, may provoke conflict between regional fractions of the working class or, again, among coalitions of classes. The current working-class espousal of regionally targeted programs for the northeastern United States may be traced to the advanced degree of capitalist development in that area. The highly skilled labor force is militantly organized to demand its share of output and a high level of social services, which, in turn, has encouraged capital to move to areas where social relations and productive forces are less well developed.

It is important to note that these aspects of the mode of production may not be territorially differentiated at all – or they may be differentiated but may not form the basis for a regional struggle. Thus, in themselves, they cannot define a region or define regionalism. A particular regional struggle may be attributable solely to one or another of these features or to a combination, but still the features do not yield an abstract definition of regionalism. If regionalism has an abstract and generalizable meaning, then it must be located in an institution or human practice other than the mode of production *per se*.

The Mode of Reproduction of People

A second human institution is the mode of reproduction of labor power[8] or, more generally, of people.[9] Like the mode of production, the reproduction of people has its social relations and forces. For most of human history, one mode of reproduction has been dominant – patriarchy. It has adapted to differences in mode of production but has been resilient in its internal structure (Rubin 1975; Hartmann 1981). Since it is less familiar than mode of production, a brief exposition is in order.

The major patriarchal institution is the household, a human social unit that generally consists of husband and wife, their children, and, in some eras, their parents and other relations. A division of labor exists whereby women labor to reproduce the labor power of both themselves and the other members of the household, either through direct production of food, clothing, and shelter, or through further processing of products or commodities produced in other workplaces (forests, fields, factories, and so on). The men generally own the household and control the most important decisions about household organization. The control of women's labor power and its products by men in households is reflected in rules and restrictions, including marriage, divorce, adultery, naming, inheritance, and alimony (in our day). It is paralleled by prohibitions and restrictions on women's ability to participate in those productive activities engaged in by men (occupational segregation) and, under capitalism, on the returns to women's labor outside the household (low wage levels for women).[10]

Preservation of patriarchal institutions or efforts to destroy them are frequently a large element in regional struggles. The "home" in the widespread sentiment "fighting for God, home, and country" euphemistically means the patriarchal household. The currently dominant faction in the nationalist struggle in Iran defends a severe patriarchy as the one primary aim of the struggle against imperialism. On the other hand, battles for liberation of a region, as in many of the socialist revolutions, include a commitment to the abolition of the worst forms of patriarchal oppression as a concession to women active in the struggle. In other cases, regional struggles have evoked a consciousness of the issue of women's liberation as a counterpart to the liberation of other groups (for example, the link between abolition and women's rights in the Civil War era). However, as in the case of the mode of production, the mode of reproduction of people does not in itself define the essence of regionalism.

Cultural Relations

Generally, neither political economists nor social scientists, nor even anthropologists, have a well-worked-out model of cultural oppression. Sociologists such as Parsons have produced models of culture, but such models are purely functionalist and do not encompass a notion of oppression. Political economists acknowledge cultural oppression and have documented it in many ap-applied studies. More recently, following Raymond Williams's (1973) pioneering theoretical work criticizing the reification of the base–superstructure dichotomy in political economy, work has begun in the political economy camp on building theoretical models of culture. For present purposes, however, I use the concept *culture* to designate one or more of those human practices, informal or formal, that are not readily identifiable as economic or political. Cultural institutions that may be important to the analysis of regionalism include language (above all), kinship groups, religious affinities, and ensembles of such cultural practices as rites of birth, death, and change of life, habits of social intercourse, or relationship to the environment.

Frequently, cultural practices that might distinguish regional groups can be traced to prior modes of production or stages in the development of productive forces.[11] An analysis of regionalism, however, cannot merely cite this historical evolution but must deal with such cultural institutions and practices on their own merits, because they demonstrate a degree of autonomy or resiliency to change that is significant in explaining contemporary social dynamics. Accepting Althusser's (1971) contention that the mode of production explains social relations only in the last instance, I contend that regionalism in many cases must be investigated in the intermediate instance, where cultural forces can be very powerful in shaping regional struggles.

To date, much of the most useful work on examining the cultural roots of regional struggles appears in the form of applied studies (for example, Buechler and Buechler 1978). This tendency toward a requirement that cultural phenomena be dealt with on a concrete, case-by-case basis may reflect not an analytical weakness but rather the fact that cultural practices vary much more across contexts than do economic or political relations. For instance, studies of Native Americans (Jorgensen 1978) show how the collective attitude toward land and its use (not exploitation) results in a regional clash between two different cultures within the current capitalist mode of production. Collins's study (1978) of Okies in the twentieth century shows that their use of family and kinship structure was extremely important in their ability to withstand dustbowl conditions, proletarian status, and migration to California during the 1930s, as well as in their contemporary coping with changes in the agricultural region of California.

Cultural practices vary from those that are nonoppressive to those that are explicitly oppressive of other groups (for example, racism). The norm against which cultural oppression is measured is the notion of self-determination: a group's right to its language, religion, and social institutions, and the right to change them as it desires, without forcible destruction or imposed change by another group. Cultural oppression may also take the form of denial of participation in existing social institutions to a particular group because of its membership or origins in a different culture.

Cultural conflicts frequently are fought along regional lines. Many regional struggles are primarily cultural in content, at least at the level of consciousness. For instance, although the division between Catholic and Protestant Ireland had its roots in the English appropriation of the best Irish

Catholic land and its settlement by English troops who had served the Crown, over generations, the struggle for an independent Ireland took on an increasingly cultural tenor, demanding freedom from the prohibition against speaking Gaelic, from restrictions on practicing the Catholic religion, and from an imposed educational system.

Nevertheless, the cultural element does not yield the fundamental definition of region. Cultural struggles may take place within regions. In the contemporary United States, however, many cultural struggles take place in urban neighborhoods and in institutions that are not regional and do not include all members of the region. Cultural struggles may also transcend territorial boundaries; a primary example was the centuries-long struggle of the Jews, in many locations in Africa, Europe, and the Middle East, to preserve Jewish culture and envision the re-creation of their homeland. Thus, regionalism is not, in essence, a cultural phenomenon.

The State, Political Oppression, and Regionalism

The final institution that is central to our analysis of regionalism is the State — that is, the political apparatus that governs a society.[12] The State is organized differently from economic and cultural institutions, in that it uses police power or the threat of it as the enforcer of its social relations (as opposed to starvation or loss of community membership). To date, the State also differs distinctly from other institutions by being territorially based, a feature that makes it central to regional analysis. State structure and dynamics differ greatly from country to country, from region to region, and from era to era. States may be oppressive, supporting the exploitation of one class by another, of one race by another, or of women by men. In the Diamond (1974) tradition, as noted earlier, the very existence of the State implies such exploitation in civil society; however, the State not only supports exploitation and oppression in other human institutions but also can be analyzed as a set of social relations itself. Such political relations, while interrelated with the social relations of modes of production, of reproduction, and of culture, have a degree of autonomy that may outlast the transition from one mode to another.

To date, political economy analysis has not met this challenge satisfactorily.[13] From Marx's time to the present, it has focused on the economic relations among people. For Marx and Engels and their nineteenth-century followers, political struggles were derivatives of economic struggles. Nevertheless, the State apparatus was a legitimate arena in which to pursue class ends, so that democracy was a rallying cry of working-class revolutionary socialism. In capitalist societies, democracy was granted, at least formally, before (and in many cases in place of) control over the means of production, fundamentally altering the arena in which class struggle took place. Subsequent to full extension of the franchise, economic conflict increasingly occurred in the State sector, through interventions such as protection and regulation of trade unions, social welfare legislation, and Keynesian attempts to manipulate the economy.

Having identified various forms of economic exploitation and cultural oppression, the question arises of whether there is a parallel phenomenon that can be identified as political oppression. This requires a commitment to a particular theory of the State, an issue not yet resolved in political economy theory. If those who argue (Poulantzas 1976) that the State is autonomous (or semiautonomous) under advanced capitalism are correct, then we can legitimately offer a notion of political oppression whereby a group's objective position is partly a function of its treatment under State structure and policy, which differs from cultural and economic relations. If we hold that the State is primarily a ruling-class institution with no social relations of its own, then political oppression is always a strict corollary to economic oppression and cannot be defined otherwise. I prefer the former characterization of the State under advanced capitalism, because it acknowledges the political gains made by the working class in the nineteenth and twentieth centuries in fighting for a democratic State that cannot avoid yielding to working-class demands in some areas, albeit reformist. From this view of the State, political oppression can be defined as the array or use of political power to deny a group the right to full participation in the political life of the community and to control over their collective future through the exercise of political mechanisms.

Although most political oppression does not take a territorial form (for example, the exclusion of the franchise to certain classes or minority groups), it may do so. The control of Native Americans through the Bureau of Indian Affairs in the past is an example. Thus, political oppression, which accompanies economic and cultural oppression, can itself be a target of struggle, as indeed it has been for Native Americans. The territorial claim to political oppression poses a moral dilemma, however, because of its nondeterminate conjunction with other forms of oppression. Autonomy for a region, or district elections replacing areawide elections, can be either progressive or regressive, depending on whose political power is enhanced by the changes and how they employ it. Although the principle of self-governance can be held in general, it may be opposed by political economists in specific cases because its net result may be to increase other forms of oppression at the same time it extends formal political rights. Lovering (1978), for instance, argues that Welsh nationalism would only benefit the Welsh capitalist class, and that Welsh workers are better off economically under British political rule. Thus, a political economy analysis must reserve normative judgment on questions of regional political oppression in the abstract. Rather, political oppression must be analyzed together with an estimation of its conjunction with economic and other forms of oppression.

A Political Economy Definition of Regionalism

Regardless of the evaluation of political oppression in a particular case of regionalism, the political dimension plays a critical role in the definition of regionalism (Markusen 1978). Even if a regional cause is solely economic in nature, its target is political, since it becomes regionalized precisely through a claim before some arm of the State to a change in territorial treatment. Thus, the State and its political relations provide the key to an abstract characterization of regionalism.

Regionalism is the political claim of a territorially identified group of people against one or several mechanisms of the State. This definition satisfies the requirements of political economy methods. First, it presents regionalism by its social relations, between a group of people and some other group, not specified in the definition, which is objectively antagonistic to some end of the first group and whose struggle occurs within the State sector. Second, it uses a territorial qualifier that distinguishes regional groups from other social groups engaged in struggle, and links territory to the existence of State institutions, so that it clearly identifies one arena of struggle — a political arena — even if the content of the struggle is economic or cultural. Third, it allows the particular delineation of the regional group to arise from historical and subjective experience, without attempting to squeeze people into an abstract ahistorical pattern of regions across the globe or to assume current forms of the State (for example, nation) as the basis of world regions.

This definition of regionalism could be applied to any era and to any mode of production. It requires only one institution — the State. Implicitly, then, the definition argues that regionalism was neither a meaningful concept nor a real experience before the emergence of the State as a political organization. Regionalism is linked fundamentally to the emergence of the State and to the particular territorial form that the State has assumed throughout recorded history. The following sections elaborate on the precision and expansiveness of this definition of regionalism.

Territoriality

The territorial nature of a regional struggle arises, in practice, from some prior differentiation between people in that region and people in other regions. The differentiation may result from various economic or cultural differences or even from differences in purely political treatment. These differences are legitimized and extended by the State, so that some social group demands better treatment or political autonomy for its territory in order to eliminate adverse sources of differentiation (for example, imperialist control over the terms of trade) or to preserve positive ones (rights to language and culture). Territorial differentiation in itself, however, is not grounds for regional definition or regional struggle. Unless the differentiation results from or is grounds for some form of oppression, regional variation in human cultures and economic structures need not provoke conflicting regional demands on the State. Furthermore, a regional cause may be oppressive, as when a regional struggle involves the attempt by one regional group to preserve its privilege or increase its exploitation of another group by insulating itself from the redistributive nature of the State (for example, the Martha's Vineyard secession drive) or by asserting monopoly control of a resource base. Thus, not all territorial struggles are progressive — a problem alluded to earlier.

Although the concept of regionalism requires territorial differentiation, the goal of a regional struggle may be the elimination of such differentiation or the end of oppression connected with it, so that that particular manifestation of regionalism may be liquidated in the process. Also, although the object of territorial struggle may be a universal claim, such as socialism or the franchise, the struggle for it may be territorially confined because the State operates within existing territorial units. Such struggles have the potential to be linked up with similar struggles by other groups.

Regional Social Relations

The social group whose circumstances and claims give the region its character may not be the entire population of that region. Frequently, a regional struggle is led by a particular group that will gain most from a particular political victory, because new policies or decentralized control of the State apparatus will permit it to pursue its class, gender, cultural, or political ends with greater success. Other members of that territorial unit may favor the existing political arrangement, because it favors them or because they fear that they will be worse off under the domination of the group leading the regional revolt. Others may participate in the regional struggle, hoping to bend it to their ends in an accompanying and successive internal struggle.

The activism suggested by the earlier definition of regionalism must not permit it to be seen as a purely subjective phenomenon. The delineation of regions is not simply subjective, based on the choices of classes and other social groups within regions. Regionalism exists not solely in the consciousness of its proponents but also in the objective political relationships existing across territories and in the political, economic, or cultural oppression that finds expression in those political relationships. The Quebecois were culturally oppressed before they began to fight back. The English-speaking population was the source of oppression, and the Canadian State was the formal means of promoting its cultural hegemony, which facilitated economic exploitation as well. The regional basis of the struggle was defined by the nature of the Canadian State, which forced the Quebecois to pursue separatism as a means of gaining cultural and political autonomy. In the course of the struggle, the boundary of the region adopted was that previously drawn in the formation of the Canadian State between the province of Quebec and other provinces, even though many French-speaking Canadians live outside this region and many English-speaking Canadians live inside it. Whether or not any conscious struggle takes place around it, territorially based differentiation, subject to political intervention or manipulation, forms the objective basis of regionalism.

The precise regional lines drawn around parties to a regional struggle will depend on alliances that can be formed with other groups that might have common cause or whose position is ambiguous but winnable.[14] Because of this, the boundary of a region may be determined by the particular nature of the struggle. In some cases, it is, itself, an object of the struggle, as when the antagonists to a regional issue wish to define the region differently in order to enhance their political or military power. An example is the central Spanish government's attempt in the mid-1970s to define the Basque region as one containing seven provinces, while the Basque separatist and nationalist movements accept only three, sometimes four; clearly, the centrists hoped that by so defining the region, they could blunt the power of the separatist movements and sway autonomy elections in their favor.

Finally, the multiple roots of regional struggles, discussed in the previous section, result in a complex pattern of social relations that can be expressed in regionalism. When class, cultural, and political claims all manifest themselves in a regional struggle, the chances are that no simple characterization of the social relations can be constructed. In these cases, multiple and competing claims over the goals of regionalism, and perhaps multiple definitions of the region, may be put forward. In Catalonia, for instance, both class and cultural identities operate in the autonomy movements; however, since some members of the Catalonian working class are Andalusian (20 percent) and thus do not speak Catalan, which is one of the political demands of the movement, they may oppose it as members of a different culture, even though Catalonian autonomy undoubtedly would further the goals of the Catalonian working class as a whole. This complexity of the social relations of regionalism requires concrete, historical analyses of each case.

The Political Claims of Regionalism

If social relations are the subject of regionalism, the political claims on the State are the object of regionalism. Regional conflicts under contemporary capitalism and the nation-state political system can be characterized by the level or severity of their claims. One type consists of regional movements that demand fundamental change in nation-state status: independent status from an existing nation-state (for example, Puerto Rico), unification with or annexation to another independent nation-state (for example, Vietnam), or cessation from one with affiliation to another (for example, Northern Ireland). A second type encompasses regions whose protagonists seek a fundamental change in the territorial structuring of power and institutions within a given nation-state, either through horizontal restructuring (such as the desire of the Upper Peninsula of Michigan to disaffiliate with Michigan and join Wisconsin) or, more importantly, through the vertical restructuring of power. This latter restructuring generally involves a decentralization of formal government machinery and decision-making power (such as autonomy movements in Quebec and Spain, the current Flemish-Walloon conflict in Belgium, proposed devolution in Scotland and Wales), but can involve a regional struggle to strengthen centralization, which would accrue to that region's advantage (for example, the Northeast's demand for federal takeover of welfare). A final type of regional conflict includes regions in which regional groups struggle within the existing political structure for more favorable treatment through State revenue collection and dispersal arrangements, expenditure programs, or rules and regulations governing the economic, cultural, or political conditions across regions. The American Sunbelt-Frostbelt or East-West struggles at the federal level exemplify this type of conflict.

The three types range from revolutionary to reform to conservative with respect to political structure but do not necessarily represent equivalent gains for regional protagonists in that order. The best strategy will depend on which classes, sectors, and so on, are represented in a particular regional movement and their relative strengths, and on which classes, and so on, control the existing and neighboring State apparatuses. The regional bourgeoisie in Scotland, Tom Nairn (1977) argues, has been better off supporting a narrowly cultural and nostalgically militaristic Scots nationalism without real ambitions to independence from England because it has profited from riding along on the coattails of British imperialism, with Scots soldiers doing much of the fighting. In contrast, the Catalonian bourgeoisie has favored strong autonomy for its region for forty years because the Franco regime denied national political power and economic privilege to the Republican-supporting Catalonians.

Working-class groups, too, may opt for different strategies toward the political content of regional demands. Lovering (1978) argues that Welsh workers would be better off eschewing the Welsh nationalist movement, which he characterizes as petit-bourgeois-based, and targeting the British State. In Catalonia and Andalusia, however, the left, working-class-based parties argue for strong worker support for regional autonomy because they feel that regional control of culture, social spending, and some forms of economic regulation are the only feasible routes toward working-class political power in Spain as a whole.

Internal disunity within a regional movement, especially a cross-class movement, frequently will express itself in disagreements about political target. Different classes will perceive that one or another type of political claim will best serve their ends. A Catalonian bourgeoisie will favor cultural autonomy and freedom from economic discrimination by the Francoist center but oppose any greater independence or any real devolution of economic power onto a regional government that is newly formed and left-dominated.

Thus, the distinction between a politically reformist and a revolutionary struggle does not carry with it any of the normative connotations that the same characterizations of economic struggles generally do in political economy thought. Since I have concluded that existence of political oppression cannot be analyzed in the absence of economic and cultural oppression, and since regional struggles are complicated by differing degrees of correspondence with class, gender, and cultural struggles, a revolutionary regional struggle is not necessarily progressive. Its quality will depend on its conjunction with other forms of existence or its elimination of oppression and exploitation.

From Regionalism to Region

Even given this view of regionalism, it is not possible to derive from it a workable political economy definition of region. The multiple sources of regional conflict and the propensity for regional boundaries and goals to change require a concrete historical analysis of each instance. A region can be conceived of in political economy as a territorial unit with some form of political status, actual or intended, but it cannot be said *a priori* to have any particular social relations or any normative status in political economy theory. This emphasis on the limited analytical content of region is important, because regions are regularly reified in both regional science and regional political economy. This section will clarify these misuses by arguing what a region is *not* in a political economy framework.

A Region Is Neither an Economic Class Nor an Economy

Two common definitions of region that are implicit in much political economy work are that a region is an economy (for example, Spain, the

Northeast) or that a region is synonymous with an economic class (for example, some applications of the internal colony argument). The first view is easy to refute, especially given the recent theoretical work on the world economic system.[15] Production and exchange in the United States are inextricably interlinked with that of the rest of the capitalist world. Furthermore, economies do not have relations – classes and political institutions within nations and regions have relations. When one region is said to be exploited by another, what is really being said is that a certain group within the first region is exploited by some group residing in the other region. Not all residents of one region benefit from the ability of a class within their region to exploit another group located in another region.[16] When theorists use regional or national designations as economies, they are generally referring to the political identity of the State, which intervenes in and governs many of the economic relationships between classes and sectors in one region and those in another.

Regions are not differentiable as classes either. At least to date, no significant one-to-one relationship between a class and a spatial location on the regional level has occurred under capitalism.[17] One way that capitalism might solve its class conflicts in the future, however, would be the regional segregation of classes – for example, assembly operators and workers in some locations and professional-managerial workers in others, as in the electronics industry currently (Saxenian 1980). It is arguable that the capitalist class has no home – that its members reside in many different places and that their profit is constantly being transformed into new production activity across locations all over the globe.

Although residents of a region may share a common source of economic exploitation (foreign ownership of land or employment as wage labor in one industry), the essence of a region is not this economic condition but rather its translation, along with other claims, into a political demand. If all the workers in Appalachia fought for control of coal production through workplace struggles, they would be fighting a class war, not a regional war. It would only coincidentally be regional; that is, it merely would take place in that region. If it included coal miners in other regions, it could be supraregional as well. The phenomenon would become regional only if this territorial differentiation became the basis for political intervention – for example, intervention from the U.S. government in the case of Appalachia, whereby coal capitalists in Appalachia might have used access to centralized political machinery to pursue their class ends. In this case, a regional struggle of coal miners against capitalists and the State would ensue: the miners' political claims against the State might include greater political autonomy for Appalachia (where workers might have greater chance to control legislatures – not the historical case) or a better deal for the region in terms of support for an alternative economic base.

The fallacy that a region is an economic unit or an economic class with a common fate is most prevalent when the internal colony thesis is applied to problem regions within advanced capitalist countries (Persky 1972; Hechter 1975). Such analysis suggests that a region may be exploited by a system of economic relationships in which other regions extract resources or products from the area; that is, the region is a colony. These treatments tend to abstract from the class, gender, and cultural relations emphasized earlier as fundamental elements in social relations among regions, implying that home ownership of resources would improve everyone's lot. In fact, miners in Butte, Montana, copper mines were no better off than Michigan copper miners when Anaconda Corporation was owned and headquartered locally. On the contrary, because of Anaconda's domination of state-level politics when it was locally based, workers actually gained political power when the company left. Economic exploitation arises from economic relationships, not territorial ones. The territorial relationship arises from the nature and extent of State intervention favoring one class or another, or one class fraction (for example, a segment of capital) at the expense of others, or a cross-class coalition at the expense of other regions. It is politically, not economically, defined. The internal colony thesis confuses class structure with State structures; it is classes that exploit classes, not places that exploit places.

A Region Is Not a Cultural Group

A similar argument may be made about cultural relations as a definer of regions. Although cultural bonds can be the content of a regional struggle, they become so only when they are translated into territorial and political terms. Black nationalism in the United States, for instance, has been an economic and cultural struggle for autonomy, but, except for the debate around a black nation in the Cotton Belt, the Marcus Garvey movement, and the settlement of Liberia, the struggle has not been regionally defined. A cultural struggle need not be currently located in a territory to be regional, but it must have a territorial aim. Thus, the Zionist vision of a Jewish State became a regional struggle even before the creation of Israel, because it laid claim to a territory and demanded an accompanying change in State structure. Similarly, the Palestinian movement is a regional struggle because it, too, claims a territory and is engaged in a political battle for it.

Cultural preservation does not require a territorial organization. Jewish culture thrives in many countries; Catholic and other cultures survive in the United States. Cultural autonomy can be fought for within a given State structure without also being territorial (or therefore regional). The right of the Amish to keep their children out of public schools, the right to bilingual education, and the civil rights of minorities all have been pursued in political arenas without being regionally based.

If a culture is territorially concentrated, it may be the basis for a regional struggle when cultural identity is suppressed by a State apparatus or used as a basis for exploitation in economic institutions. The possibility for a territorial solution may result in migration of cultural refugees to a place where the neighborhood, the enclave, the region, or even the nation can provide cultural protection through control of a separate political apparatus or spatially differential political treatment. American history is replete with such examples, from the original religious colonies to the Mormon settlement of Utah and the minority migration patterns across regions. Culturally based regions can also be imposed, as in the forced enclosure of Native Americans on reservations in the western United States (even if they were originally eastern groups) or in controls on migration of certain groups internally. Cultural struggles become regional when the members of the culture are territorially concentrated and differentiated (or wish to be), and when they pursue cultural ends through political channels, arguing for a territorial, rather than universal, solution.

The Region Is Not Solely a Political Unit

I have argued that economic and cultural conflicts may not be regional and that regional struggles can be either economic or cultural. Thus, regions cannot be defined abstractly as either economic or cultural phenomena. It is now necessary to argue that regions are not solely political units and that not all political units constitute regions. The definition of regionalism implies only that regions are territorial units, with some political content to the definition. The political dimension is essential to the definition, whereas economic and cultural content are not. Although it is possible to argue, however, that a regional struggle, in addition to having a political focus, may be predominantly political in content (against political oppression), it is also necessary to point out that the nature of political oppression must ultimately be bound up with some form of economic or cultural oppression, arising from differentiation across regions.

First, it is true that all political units forming the basis of the State are territorial, at least currently. Not all political organizations are territorial, however; some (such as the Trilateral Commission and the Fourth International) transcend existing political delineations because they are internationalist in vision. State machinery is arrayed on a territorial basis, however, with nations and their political subdivisions as the major units. This is a historical product of the nature of State power (police power and violence being most easily extended and defended territorially, at least in the era of armies dependent on human labor power) and of the evolution of capitalism, in which large-scale production, a world market, and the competitive and chaotic but insistent growth intrinsic to capitalist development promoted the emergence of the nation-state.

Since territoriality is merely a feature of the evolution, it is in no sense absolute or ahistorical. It may disappear in the future, when we might imagine the State organized on lines other than territorial; or a multinational State may replace the current multiplicity of States. Even currently, the strength of the territorial characterization varies tremendously across nations in which subnational political units have different degrees of autonomy, power and, therefore, significance. In the federal nations of the United States and Canada, the states and provinces (themselves the product of strong prior regions in the nation-building process) have considerably more autonomy than provinces in European nations, where class-based voting is more prevalent. Even in countries where no well-developed subnational political machinery exists, however, regional claims are still regional when they demand territorially based treatment (for example, Welsh and Scottish nationalism).

On the other hand, not every territory or every political unit constitutes a region. The existence of one or more sources of differentiation around which regional struggle potentially or actually forms is a sufficient condition. The Navajo nation is a region because it has a territorial basis and holds political claims on both state and federal governments; the Navajo culture and its evolution from a prior mode of production are what lend it its identity. In addition, regional boundaries are not given solely by existing political boundaries. The northeastern United States is a region because it is currently experiencing a form of economic decline that differentiates it from the rest of the country and because a cross-class coalition residing there now levies political claims for favorable territorial treatment on the federal government. Its boundaries, however, are not precisely defined. It is variously represented by the New England Congressional Caucus, a narrow definition; by the Coalition of Northeastern Governors (CONEG), a broader definition; and by the Northeast-Midwest Institute, a research arm and the broadest definition. Each of these is an attempt not only to broaden alliances but also to define the region to correspond to a particular economic experience.

Implications For Research On Regional Development

The foregoing discussion suggests several conclusions for the political economy analysis of regional development. First, the argument that, for political economists, regions do not exist as an abstract category implies that regional development cannot be discussed or studied abstractly. Regions do not develop; social relations within regions and across regions develop. Theorizing about the course of capitalist development within a region requires an empirical analysis that identifies the cultural, political, and economic structures that have evolved historically, both internally and with respect to other regions. In this respect, it is likely that regional political economists will not be able to do as well as urban political economists have done in identifying and analyzing the process of urbanization under capitalism.[18] There simply is no counterpart regionalization that appears intrinsic to even one stage of capitalist evolution.

Second, regional political economists should attempt to make their analyses more rigorous by eschewing the fetishism of space — that is, the treatment of regions as if they were synonymous with economic classes, economies, or cultural groups. The political economy literature on development, regionalism, and even urbanism is replete with such usages.

Finally, the political nature of regionalism and regions requires that any analysis of regionalism incorporate a theory of the State and a study of its concrete presence in a particular regional context. The greatest weaknesses in regional and international analyses of capitalist development are (1) the absence of any explicit theory of the State and (2) the failure to distinguish between economic and political relations.

Notes

1. Here and throughout, the capitalized *State* is used to refer to the Marxian characterization of the entire political apparatus in a capitalist society, while the word *state* refers to American subfederal political entities.

2. This is not true of regional science, which has produced an extensive if inconclusive literature on the definition of region. See appendix 1, "Social Science Definitions of Region," in the author's forthcoming book, *Regional Political Economy.*

3. It is assumed throughout this chapter that the terms *region* and *regional* apply to any bounded and definite territory larger than a labor market area — that is, an SMSA. Metropolitan units, small towns, and neighborhoods are given the description *city* and *urban*. Note that this delineation includes everything from a province or state to a nation or set of nations, such as the EEC, and territorial units without formal political existence, such as Appalachia. This usage comes from common practice (in urban and regional planning) and captures only the physical dimension of the terms. It is not a substantive definition, which is the subject of the subsequent sections.

4. One version of the argument contends that a political economy analysis does not require that mode of production be the primary human social relation that characterizes a society (Hartmann and Markusen 1980). This argument holds that it is erroneous to assume abstractly that there must be one dominant set of social relations in any society in any era. For instance, many analyses of capitalism ignore or belittle the continuation of patriarchy and the exploitation of women's labor power in the patriarchal household, coincident with exploitation of wage labor, on the grounds that such exploitation is subordinate to, or even caused by, capitalist exploitation. A similar argument regarding culture may be found in Collins (1978).

5. Some political economists contend that the very existence of institutions signals exploitation and oppression, since otherwise there would be no need for them, as in the theory of the withering away of the State. Although this position is attractive, especially when it is argued forcefully by scholars such as Stanley Diamond (1974), I prefer not to employ this restrictive definition of institution, contending that nonexploitative social organizations with a division of labor may indeed exist.

6. Both exploitation and oppression refer to forms of alienation. Exploitation generally refers to the appropriation of labor power or other economic resources. Oppression is a more general term, which can include the appropriation and domination of other forms of human activity and resources, whereby one group controls a set of institutions that determine the content of human experience at the expense of another group.

7. It is assumed to be unnecessary here to explain the mode of production and the specific types that have been identified empirically by Marxist scholars. See Hobsbaum (1964), Foster-Carter (1978) and Balibar (1971).

8. In contemporary society, the dominant ideologies label this sphere of human activity consumption (see any economics textbook). This characterization profoundly misunderstands the organization of the household and the expenditure of labor time within it under both modern capitalism and previous modes of production (Hartmann and Markusen 1980).

9. Even the use of the term *labor power* accepts the categories of the prior analysis of mode of production. In order to see household labor as producing not just labor power but the whole human being, I prefer to use the rather odd term *reproduction of people*.

10. Numerous attempts have been made to subordinate the contemporary social relations of household production into the political economy analysis of the capitalist mode of production (Harrison 1973; Secombe 1974; Rowbotham 1973; Zaretsky 1973; Quick 1972; Smith 1975). I side with the feminist critics (Hartmann 1979; Rubin 1975; Eisenstein 1979), who argue that patriarchy constitutes a separate, though interrelated, system of social relations that involves different forums for struggle (especially the household) and champions different issues (child care, health care, reproductive rights, neighborhood issues, and so forth).

11. Some excellent attempts have been made to show how various cultural institutions are derived from the rise or fall of a mode of production, from patriarchy, or from a more detailed division of labor. See Levi-Strauss (1969) on kinship, V. Gordon Childe (1965) on cultural generality, and Imamu Baraka (1963) on American jazz.

12. In order to deal with the State more rigorously, this definition excludes many of the cultural institutions sometimes included under the rubric "State." The State is that identifiable set of institutions that organize and intervene in all other aspects of social life, codified in law and backed by the threat of police power. This discussion refers exclusively to the State as it exists under predominantly capitalist modes of production.

13. The new generation of political economists dealing with theories of the State, however, is rapidly approaching such an analysis (O'Connor 1973; Bridges 1974; Poulantzas 1976; Wolfe 1977).

14. This imprecision is similar to the problem of drawing class lines in revolutionary struggles, such as in China, or the problem of delineating the working class – for example, whether it includes professionals.

15. Ironically, this same literature perpetuates the confusion by continuing to use the same language (Wallerstein 1974; Kay 1975).

16. However, the exploiting class may permit the other residents of its region to appropriate some gains through the struggle among groups in that region. See the Emmanuel and Bettelheim (1970) debate over whether workers in capitalist countries exploit Third World workers.

17. In urban areas, one can make an argument about class segregation across space (Markusen 1976). The closest analogies at the regional level are mining communities, such as Cripple Creek,

Colorado, Lead, South Dakota, and Appalachia, but even these had some independent mine owners, entrepreneurs, and local merchant capitalists.

18. See, for instance, Tabb and Sawers (1978), Castells (1977), Cox (1978), Pickvance (1976), Harloe (1977), and issues of the *International Journal of Urban and Regional Research* (1977).

References

Allen, Robert. 1976. "Racism and the Black Nation Thesis." *Socialist Revolution* 27 (January-March).

Althusser, Louis. 1971. "The Object of Capital." In *Reading Capital,* edited by Louis Althusser and Etienne Balibar. New York: Pantheon.

Arthur, C. J. 1970. Introduction to *The German Ideology,* by Karl Marx and Friedrich Engels. New York: International Publishers.

Balibar, Etienne. 1971. "From Periodization to Modes of Production." In *Reading Capital,* edited by Louis Althusser and Etienne Balibar. New York: Pantheon.

Baraka, Imamu Amiri. 1963. *Blues People: Negro Music in White America.* New York: Morrow.

Bridges, Amy. 1974. "Nicos Poulantzas and the Marxist Theory of the State." *Politics and Society* 2 (Winter).

Buechler, Hans, and Buechler, Judith. 1978. "Social Class, Conflict, and Unequal Development in Spanish Galicia." *Review of Radical Political Economics* 10:130-135.

Castells, Manuel. 1977. *The Urban Question: A Marxist Approach* (trans. Alan Sheridan). Cambridge, Mass.: MIT Press.

Childe, V. Gordon. 1965. *Man Makes Himself,* 4th ed. London: Watts.

Collins, Linda. 1978. "Okies in Socio-Historical Perspective." Working Paper, Department of Sociology, University of California, Berkeley.

Cox, Kevin, Ed. 1978. *Urbanization and Conflict in Market Societies.* Chicago: Maaroufa Press.

Davis, Horace. 1967. *Nationalism and Socialism.* New York: Monthly Review Press.

Diamond, Stanley. 1974. *In Search of the Primitive: A Critique of Civilization.* New Brunswick, N.J.: Transaction Books.

Domhoff, G. William. 1979. *The Powers That Be.* New York: Random House.

Eisenstein, Zillah R. 1979. *Capitalist Patriarchy and the Case for Socialist Feminism.* New York: Monthly Review Press.

Emmanuel, Arghiri, and Bettelheim, Charles. 1970. "International Solidarity of Workers: Two Views." *Monthly Review* (June).

Foster-Carter, Aidan. 1978. "The Modes of Production Controversy." *New Left Review* 107.

Gaventa, John, and Couto, Richard. 1976. *"Appalachia and the Third Face of Power."* Working Paper, Department of Political Science, Vanderbilt University.

Gutman, Herbert. 1976a. *The Black Family in Slavery and Freedom, 1750–1925.* New York: Pantheon.

______. 1976b. *Work, Culture, and Society in Industrializing America: Essays in American Working Class and Social History:* New York: Knopf.

Harloe, Michael, Ed. 1977. *Captive Cities: Studies in the Political Economy of Cities and Regions.* London and New York: Wiley.

Harrison, John. 1973. "The Political Economy of Housework." *Bulletin of the Conference of Socialist Economists* (Winter), pp. 35–52.

Hartmann, Heidi. 1981. "The Family as the Focus of Gender, Class, and Political Struggle: The Example of Housework." *Signs,* Vol. 6, No. 3: 366–94.

Hartmann, Heidi, and Markusen, Ann. 1980. "Contemporary Marxist Theory and Practice: A Feminist Critique." *Review of Radical Political Economics* 12.

Hechter, Michael. 1975. *Internal Colonialism: The Celtic Fringe in British National Development.* London: Routledge and Kegan Paul.

Hobsbaum, Eric. 1964. Introduction to *Precapitalist Economic Formations,* by Karl Marx (trans. Jack Cohen). London: Lawrence and Wishart.

International Journal of Urban and Regional Research 1–3. 1977–1979. London: Edward Arnold.

Jorgensen, Joseph. 1978. "A Century of Political Economic Effects on American Indian Society: 1880–1980." *Journal of Ethnic Studies* 6.

Kay, Geoffrey. 1975. *Development and Underdevelopment: A Marxist Analysis.* London: Macmillan.

Levi-Strauss, Claude. 1969. *The Elementary Structures of Kinship* (trans. James Harle Bell), edited by John Richard von Sturmer and Rodney Needham, rev. ed. Boston: Beacon Press.

Lovering, John. 1978. "The Theory of the 'Internal Colony' and the Political Economy of Wales." *Review of Radical Political Economics* 10: 55–67.

Markusen, Ann R. 1976. "Class and Urban Social Expenditures: A Local Theory of the State." *Kapitalistate* 4–5.

______. 1978. "Regionalism and the Capitalist State: The Case of the United States." *Kapitalistate* 7.

______. *Regional Political Economy.* Unpublished manuscript.

Nairn, Tom. 1977. *The Break-up of Britain: Crisis and Neo-Nationalism.* London: New Left Books.

O'Connor, James. 1973. *The Fiscal Crisis of the State.* New York: St. Martin's Press.

______. 1978. "The Democratic Movement in the United States." *Kapitalistate* 7.

Offe, Claus. 1972. "Advanced Capitalism and the Welfare State." *Politics and Society* 2.

Persky, Joe. 1972. "Regional Colonialism and the Southern Economy." *Review of Radical Political Economy* 4: 70–79.

Pickvance, C.S., Ed. 1976. *Urban Sociology: Critical Essays.* New York: St. Martin's Press.

Poulantzas, Nicos. 1976. *Political Power and Social Classes* (trans. and ed. Timothy O'Hagan). London: New Left Books.

Quick, Paddy. 1972. "Women's Work." *The Review of Radical Political Economics* 4(Summer): 2.

Review of Radical Political Economics 10. 1978. Special Issue on Regional Uneven Development in Advanced Capitalism.

______. 12. 1980. Special Issue on the Soviet Union.

Rowbotham, Sheila. 1973. *Women's Consciousness, Man's World.* London: Penguin.

Rubin, Gayle. 1975. "The Traffic in Women: Notes on the 'Political Economy' of Sex." In *Toward an Anthropology of Women,* edited by Rayna Reiter. New York: Monthly Review Press.

Saxenian, Annalee. 1980. *"Silicon Chips and Spatial Structure: The Semiconductor Industry and Urbanization in Santa Clara County, California."* Master's thesis, University of California, Berkeley.

Secombe, Wally. 1974. "The Housewife and Her Labor Under Capitalism." *New Left Review* (January-February), pp. 3-24.

Smith, Dorothy. 1975. "Women, the Family, and Corporate Capitalism." *Berkeley Journal of Sociology* 20: 55-90.

Soja, Edward. 1978. " 'Topian' Marxism and Spatial Praxis: A Reconsideration of the Political Economy of Space." Working Paper, School of Architecture and Planning, University of California, Los Angeles.

Stone, Michael, and Hartmann, Chester. 1980. "Housing: A Marxist Analysis and Socialist Program." In *Urban and Regional Planning in an Age of Austerity,* edited by Pierre Clavel, William Goldsmith, and John Forester. New York: Pergamon Press.

Tabb, William, and Sawers, Larry. 1978. *Marxism and the Metropolis.* New York: Oxford University Press.

Thompson, E.P. 1963. *The Making of the English Working Class.* London: Victor Gollancz.

Vilar, Pierre. 1979. "On Nations and Nationalism" (trans. Elizabeth Fox Genovese). *Marxist Perspectives* 2(Spring): 8-29.

Wallerstein, Immanuel. 1974. *The Modern World System.* New York: Academic Press.

Williams, Raymond. 1973. "Base and Superstructure in Marxist Cultural History." *New Left Review* 82 (November-December).

Wolfe, Alan. 1977. *The Limits of Legitimacy.* New York: Free Press.

Zaretsky, Eli. 1973. "Capitalism, the Family, and Personal Life." *Socialist Revolution,* no. 1-2.

5 COMMODITY PRODUCTION AND INTERREGIONAL TRANSFERS OF VALUE

Panagis Liossatos

This chapter is concerned with the question of uneven appropriation of the net social product by regionally based fractions of capital. We therefore propose to examine just a moment in the process of uneven regional development. Unfortunately, we shall not offer any direct integration of uneven regional development with capitalist accumulation. We intend to work out only some of the theoretical preconditions for doing so. Specifically, we shall elaborate a concept of regional inequalities at a level of abstraction at which accumulation is absent and the capital-labor relation is reproduced on the same scale from year to year (simple reproduction). This is an abstraction that provides the minimum theoretical structure required for the analysis of value-price relationships and for the introduction of the concept of unequal interregional relations. This method of investigation emanates from Marx (1977, Ch. 23) and Sraffa (1960).

Marx's (1967, Ch. 9) treatment of value-price relationships is undoubtedly incomplete and approximate; yet it is still the most promising point of departure for the investigation of unequal relations beneath the surface equality of the market, such as transfers of economic value from *peripheral* to *core* regions. Specifically, Marx's important suggestion is that the very condition of equality among competing capitals – the formation of a uniform rate of profit in all branches of production – effects an uneven distribution of the mass of surplus value among capitalists. Thus, firms in sectors of higher (lower) value composition of capital than society's average realize greater (lesser) profits than their respective contribution to the mass of surplus value.

Once the concept of production branch or sector is taken to be logically prior to that of region, one can, in principle, translate intersectoral into interregional transfers of value. This is, in fact, the method adopted in this chapter. Thus, unequal interregional relations are derived from a determinate territorial division of labor. It should be noted, however, that this is a meaningful procedure only in the context of considering a snapshot of the multiregion structure of the economy and the conditions of its simple reproduction. The matter is not so simple when accumulation proper is introduced. The dialectical interaction between capitalist accumulation and territorial division of labor must be theorized (see Massey 1978).

Even at the level of simple reproduction, however, theoretical difficulties still persist. It is a standard practice, for example, to identify all types of unequal exchange as value-price discrepancies.[1] Generally, however, such an identification is erroneous. The well-known deviations by prices of production from labor values are perfectly consistent with equal exchange – namely, the exchange of equivalents. To see this, we must carefully consider Marx's theory of value – focusing on the unity of the substance of value (abstract labor) and its monetary form – and restructure accordingly earlier and recent conceptions of the transformation problem.[2] This we shall do by modifying and reinterpreting Sraffa's (1960) theory of price in the light of Marx's theory of value and money.

It turns out that there is no place or need for any notion of unequal exchange in the resulting framework. On the contrary, it is equivalent exchange that reproduces unequal interregional relations. These relations are identified not by examining value-price discrepancies but by comparing each region's contribution to and actually realized share in society's monetary income. Hence, transfers of value from one region to another are expressed as transfers of purchasing power over the net social product.

It should be stressed at this point that the rejection of the standard notion of unequal exchange on our part has no direct bearing on Emmanuel's conception of unequal exchange in the broad or strict sense. That conception is beyond the scope of this analysis. Despite a widespread misinterpretation, unequal exchange is not expressed in terms of value-price deviations in the Emmanuel system (Emmanuel 1972, pp. 324–325).

This chapter first develops a theoretical framework for the analysis of value-price relations using a simple two-sector model, and then takes up the question of regional inequalities.

Sraffian Prices in the Light of Marx's Theory of Value and Money

The intent of this section is to develop a conceptual framework for the analysis of unequal interregional relations. To avoid complex formalism, we shall present the main ideas with the aid of a simple two-sector model. For a more complete mathematical treatment and multisectoral analysis, the reader is referred to Liossatos (1980a, 1980b).

Imagine a purely capitalist society consisting of only two antagonistic social classes – capitalists and workers – to be referred to hereafter as "the society." Suppose that, during a typical production cycle – taken to be a year – this society produces only two distinct use-values, iron and corn. Specifically, it produces x_i tons of iron by means of x_{ii} tons of iron and L_i man-hours of human labor. At the same time, it produces x_c bushels of corn by means of x_{ic} tons of iron and L_c man-hours of human labor. The annual productive activity of the society is given by the following two processes:

$$(x_{ii}, 0, L_i) \rightarrow x_i \tag{5.1}$$

and

$$(x_{ic}, 0, L_c) \rightarrow x_c \tag{5.2}$$

where the zeros in expressions (5.1) and (5.2) indicate that corn is not an input in the production of iron and corn. Iron symbolizes a machine or capital good, but it is a peculiar machine in that its lifespan is assumed to be one year – that is, it is completely used up during a single production period. In other words, fixed capital is assumed away. It is also assumed that natural resources (land, mineral deposits, and so forth) are free goods, that transportation costs for both intraregional and interregional shipments are zero, and that the society does not trade with the outside world. Further, it is posited that the national territory within which the society exists is divided into two determinate regions, characterized by complete specialization in the production of one use-value. We can then identify them as the iron and corn regions, specializing in expressions (5.1) and (5.2), respectively. In addition to intraregional trade, there is a clear necessity for interregional trade: the iron region needs corn for capitalist and worker's consumption, while the corn region cannot carry out production without importing iron. Finally, it is assumed that not only iron and corn but also money capital and labor can move freely from one region to another, as is characteristic of full competition.

As noted earlier, all the foregoing assumptions and the confinement of the analysis to a situation of simple reproduction (to be discussed shortly) should be judged not on the basis of their realism but rather on whether or not they define an appropriate level of abstraction in reference to the issues under investigation.

Simple reproduction refers to a situation in which the system of expressions (5.1) and (5.2) repeats itself from one year to the next without any change. The Sraffian prices of reproduction are defined as the prices that if adopted by the market, make this process of reproduction possible. Accordingly, the prices of reproduction ensure that capitalists in each region receive sufficient revenues from selling their products by the end of a production cycle (where, by assumption, the market opens) to repurchase the means of production used up during the year, to pay wages to ensure labor for the next period, and to make a profit. Further, prices must be consistent with rules of distribution as determined by full competition: a uniform rate of profit (r) and wage rate (w) in both regions. Thus, we are concerned with the simple reproduction of an equilibrium state, defined as that state of the economy in which there is no movement of money capital or labor from or into any region.

If p_i and p_c denote the prices of iron and corn, respectively, the conditions of simple reproduction of an equilibrium are as follows:

$$p_i x_i = (1+r) p_i x_{ii} + w L_i \tag{5.3}$$

and

$$p_c x_c = (1+r) p_i x_{ic} + w L_c \tag{5.4}$$

where we have adopted the convention that wages are paid from revenue by the end of the year rather than being advanced in the beginning of the year.

The system of simultaneous equations (5.3) and (5.4) constitutes the basic statement of Sraffa's theory of price in the context of our model. For a detailed investigation of the properties of such a system, see, for example, Harris (1978, Ch. 4). Here we need only those properties that are relevant for our argument.

The exogenous data in equations (5.3) and (5.4) are the parameters that characterize the technology or the production technique as depicted by the methods of production or processes in expressions (5.1) and (5.2) in the iron and corn region, respectively. The unknowns are the prices of iron and corn and the two distributive variables, the profit and wage rates. Because equations (5.3) and (5.4) can determine only relative prices, we may select corn, for example, as the numeraire by setting $p_c = 1$. Then both the price of iron and the wage rate are expressed in terms of corn (in this case, w is referred to as the real wage rate), but we are still left with two equations and three unknowns. One distributive variable must be specified exogenously. Hence, for a given technology, the distribution of income determines the relative price of iron, not vice versa, as would be the case in neoclassical theory.

An important relation implied by equations (5.3) and (5.4) is a wage-profit trade-off: the real wage rate is determined as a decreasing function of the rate of profit. Thus, any increase in the rate of profit is accompanied by a decrease in the real wage rate. Accordingly, the wage-profit trade-off is a relation of distribution expressing the conflict between capitalist and workers over the distribution of the economic pie – that is, the net social product per year.

The net social product is obtained by subtracting from the gross social product, here consisting of the gross outputs of iron (x_i) and corn (x_c), the quantities of iron and corn used up in annual production. To simplify – given that there is no growth in our model – we may posit that the gross output x_i of iron is completely used up during a production cycle; that is,

$$x_i = x_{ii} + x_{ic} \tag{5.5}$$

Hence, the annual net output of iron is zero. Further, since corn is not used in production, the entire gross output x_c of corn is available as net output by the end of each production cycle. Therefore, x_c represents the net social product per year. Consequently, the social (or national) income Y is given by

$$Y = p_c x_c \tag{5.6}$$

As expected, Y is distributed between profits (rK) and wages (wL), where

$$K = p_i(x_{ii} + x_{ic}) \tag{5.7}$$

is the flow of social (circulating) capital and

$$L = L_i + L_c \tag{5.8}$$

is total labor employed annually. In fact, from equations (5.3) to (5.8), one can easily derive the familiar income identity:

$$Y = rK + wL \tag{5.9}$$

Note that, from now on, we no longer adhere to any particular numeraire.

It is useful at this point to derive the regional counterparts of equation (5.9). The annual income of a region is defined as the difference between regional revenue and the cost of replacing the means of production used up in regional production. If Y_i and Y_c denote the incomes of the iron and corn regions, respectively, then, from equations (5.3) and (5.4) we have

$$Y_i = rK_i + wL_i \tag{5.10}$$

and

$$Y_c = rK_c + wL_c \tag{5.11}$$

where

$$K_i = p_i x_{ii} \quad \text{and} \quad K_c = p_i x_{ic} \tag{5.12}$$

are quantities of circulating capital in the respective regions. Equations (5.10) and (5.11) state that regional income equals the sum of regional profits plus regional wages. It is easy to verify that

$$Y = Y_i + Y_c \tag{5.13}$$

It is now apparent that social production in the Sraffa system is identified as a process of production of use-values. Relations of distribution are externally superimposed on the production technique. There is no conception of value creation as an integral aspect of social production. As a consequence, one can speak, for example, of regional incomes realized but cannot define regional contributions to the net social product and social income. Therefore, one cannot decipher unequal interregional relations in a purely Sraffian framework.

What we must do next is replace the intuitive, untheorized notions of commodities, capitalism, profits, and so forth, in the Sraffa system by the Marxian concept of capitalist commodity production. At the most abstract level, capitalism is characterized by commodity production – that is, private production not for own use but for sale on a market. Private labor, therefore, is not directly social. It becomes social through exchange, which transforms use-values into quantities of worth (values) and homogenizes the concrete private labor that produced them. Market exchange is grasped theoretically as "a social process by which the products of independent private labors are integrated with one another and form fractions of society's overall labor" (Aglietta 1979, p. 40). This homogeneous character of labor as fraction of social labor is called abstract labor.

We can now see that the notion of labor inputs (L_i and L_c) in expressions (5.1) and (5.2) is problematic. If L_i and L_c are viewed as technical inputs or concrete labors, they are not commensurable and, hence, the addition in equation (5.8) does not make any sense.[3] Anticipating the process of exchange and assuming that whatever is produced via expressions (5.1) and (5.2) is sold, we can identify L_i and L_c as abstract labor – that is, as portions of society's overall annual labor L, expressed in hours of work performed during the year, regardless of specialization. Only in this context does the addition in equation (5.8) become meaningful. Then, however, expressions (5.1) and (5.2) can no longer be interpreted as pure technology. By positing that whatever is produced finds a buyer, we essentially imply that expressions (5.1) and (5.2) specify not only methods of production but also conditions of social demand. Thus, the two expressions, together with two additional givens, to be defined later, constitute conditions of production and exchange as observed during a typical year. It is generally impossible to separate social from technical relations or features of production from those of circulation within these conditions. However, a partial separation will be preserved in the hypothetical society under discussion because of neo-Ricardian elements that undoubtedly remain in our theoretical setting – for example, the specification of expressions (5.1) and (5.2) in physical terms.

Having introduced the concept of abstract labor, we can now express quantitatively the homogenization of products as commodities (values)[4] by the following equations:

$$\lambda_i x_i = \lambda_i x_{ii} + L_i \qquad (5.14)$$

and

$$\lambda_c x_c = \lambda_i x_{ic} + L_c \tag{5.15}$$

where λ_i and λ_c are the values (or labor values) of iron and corn, respectively. In general – as can be seen from equations (5.14) and (5.15) – the value of a commodity is not embodied labor but rather the portion of social labor that is socially necessary for the reproduction of one unit of that commodity. "Socially necessary" implies (1) that the conditions of production involved in expressions (5.1) and (5.2) are socially dominant (or average) and (2) that produced outputs reflect social demand (so that whatever is produced finds a buyer and, hence, L_i and L_c are validated as fractions of social labor).[5] Again, we see why expressions (5.1) and (5.2) should be interpreted as conditions of production and exchange in a Marxian setting. For example, the net output x_c of corn must coincide with the social demand for corn (capitalist and worker's consumption) for the subscripts i and c in equations (5.14) and (5.15) to be identified as the values of iron and corn, respectively.

As expected, the value $\lambda_c x_c$ of the net social product x_c equals social labor L performed per year; that is,

$$\lambda_c x_c = L \tag{5.16}$$

which can be derived from equations (5.5), (5.8), and the system of equations (5.14) and (5.15). Hence, society's overall annual labor is the value that the society creates per year. Commodity production is the unity of a labor process (production of use-values) and a process of value creation, the process of value creation being the dominant element.

The definition of the Marxian concept of value would be incomplete, however, if we were to specify only its substance (abstract labor) and magnitude without considering its form. In fact, products of labor become commodities (values) – that is, quanta of social labor – only when exchanged for a sum of money. The unit of measurement of value is not labor-time, as it might appear, but is determined by the social practice of exchange. It is that exchange practice that establishes a socially sanctioned yardstick (universal equivalent) for the measurement of value: money. Value is inseparable from its monetary form. Marx's (1977) remarks on this matter are unequivocal:

> It is one of the chief failings of classical political economy that it has never succeeded, by means of its analysis of commodities, and in particular of their value, in discovering the form of value which in fact turns value into exchange value. Even its best representatives, Adam Smith and Ricardo, treat the form of value as something of indifference, something external to the nature of the commodity itself. . . . We therefore find that economists who are entirely agreed that labor-time is the measure of the magnitude of value, have the strangest and most contradictory ideas about money, that is, about the universal equivalent in its finished form. (p. 174)

Marx's critique is directly applicable to those contemporary theories that posit the real side of the economy to be the realm of relative prices (exchange ratios of use-values) and introduce money as an external quantity for the determination of the level of prices. Some of the difficulties surrounding the transformation problem arise precisely from the fact that both Marx's own treatment and post-Marxian discussions of the problem abstract from money and resort to arbitrary numeraire selection or invariance postulates.[6]

The need of private labor to be socially validated in a commodity economy operates on independent producers as a monetary constraint. Specifically, this constraint requires that the total income of society Y be the monetary expression of the value L created annually by the society; that is,

$$Y = mL \tag{5.17}$$

where m is the monetary expression of the working hour. As the conditions of production and exchange remain invariant in simple reproduction, we take m as an exogenously given constant. When all commodities produced according to expressions (5.1) and (5.2) successfully complete their metamorphoses and become use-values for either productive or private consumption, the social value L is realized in money, the total income of society.[7] This is the meaning of equation (5.17). In other words, the annual outcome of commodity production is not only the net product (x_c) but also value L, which is the substance of society's purchasing power (social income Y) over the net product.

The concept of value (substance, magnitude, and form of value) expresses the relations of a commodity-producing society – the relations of private production. This society, however, is neither logically[8] nor historically a self-reproducible form of division of labor. It is merely an abstraction, the first stage for the analysis of the capitalist mode of production. In fact, that mode of production is defined as a commodity-producing society in which social labor becomes wage labor. Accordingly, the relations characteristic of capitalism consist not only of private production but also of the appropriation of the ensemble of conditions of production by one section of society and the simultaneous transformation of the other section into a wage-earning class. These two features of the capitalist mode of production are captured by the concept of capital or the capital relation, which is defined as "the social relation of appropriation, as commodities, of products of labor and labor-power sold by *free* individuals" (Aglietta 1979, p. 46).

The capital relation is expressed in terms of value as a division of the annual production of value (L) into the value of labor-power (V), reflecting the cost of reproduction of the wage earners, and the mass of surplus value (S) that is appropriated by the capitalist class as a whole. In symbols,

$$L = V + S \tag{5.18}$$

The degree of exploitation of labor by capital is measured by the social rate of surplus value *e*, where

$$e = \frac{S}{V} \tag{5.19}$$

Accordingly, capitalist commodity production is the unity of a labor process and a process of valorization (value and surplus value creation), where the valorization process is the dominant element.

Normally, the rate of surplus value is treated as a dependent variable whose magnitude is determined by the length of the working day, the intensity and productivity of labor, and so forth. Thus, *e* is generally an expression of social and technical relations, which are inseparable from each other. However, in the setting of simple reproduction, it is harmless and illuminating to reverse the order of things and take *e* as an exogenous datum. This exogeneity of *e* amounts to taking the balance of class forces (capitalists and workers) as exogenous (Roemer 1978). It is a useful device for making transparent the relationship between *e* and the monetary rate of profit (*r*), thus showing that surplus value is the substance of capitalist profits. We should keep in mind, however, that such a separation of social relations from material conditions is completely inappropriate for the study of accumulation.

The realization of surplus value as profit presupposes and is effected through the realization of value (the monetary constraint). The realization of value, however, is not sufficient to integrate capitalist production and circulation. In addition, we should specify how *V* and *S* are transformed to wages (*W*) and profits (*P*), respectively. Our basic results are not affected (Liossatos 1980b) if we ignore the complications of collective labor bargaining and posit

$$W = mV \tag{5.20}$$

which, in view of equations (5.17), (5.18), and

$$Y = P + W \tag{5.21}$$

yields

$$P = mS \tag{5.22}$$

Equations (5.20) and (5.22) state that wages (*W*) and profits (*P*) are the monetary expressions of the value of labor-power (*V*) and surplus value (*S*), respectively. These are more precise statements of such familiar expressions as "social labor power is sold at its value" and "the sum total of profits is equal to the mass of surplus value." Since the wage rate (*w*) is the ratio W/L, and because of equations (5.18) and (5.19), equation (5.20) yields

$$w = \frac{m}{(1+e)} \tag{5.23}$$

Thus, we obtain a modified Sraffa system composed of the price equations (5.3) and (5.4), the distributive specification in equation (5.23) and the monetary constraint in equation (5.17), which, in view of equation (5.6), reads

$$p_c x_c = mL \tag{5.24}$$

In this enlarged model, the coefficients in expressions (5.1) and (5.2), the monetary expression of the working hour, and the social rate of surplus value (e) constitute exogenous data; these are not merely technical methods of production but an ensemble of sociotechnical conditions of production and exchange as observed for a typical year. The four equations (5.3), (5.4), (5.23), and (5.24) allow us to determine the four endogenous variables: the wage (w) and profit (r) rates and the prices of iron (p_i) and corn (p_c).

The preceding enlargement of the Sraffa system is essentially an embedding of Sraffa's theory of price in Marx's theory of value, surplus value, and money, which comes about through a movement from the level of abstraction of the capital relation to that of competition. At the level of the capital relation, the two antagonistic classes are treated as homogeneous entities without internal differentiation and intraclass competition. This is a legitimate abstraction, because the capital relation is the fundamental structural force that conditions everything else (income distribution, competition, prices, and so forth) in the capitalist mode of production. Hence, the capital relation is logically prior to the relations of competition – a lower level of abstraction, where intraclass fragmentation and competition (for both capitalists and workers) is introduced. The price equations (5.3) and (5.4) – the original Sraffa system – pertain precisely to that level. They express the effect of competition: the equalization of wage and profit rates. Adjoining equations (5.23) and (5.24) to the price equations (5.3) and (5.4) amounts to grounding competition, income distribution, and prices on the capital relation. As a consequence, relations between things (rate of profit, wage rate, and prices) are grasped theoretically as relations between people.

This is, in fact, the meaning of the transformation of value into monetary magnitudes that is implicit in the system of equations (5.3), (5.4), (5.23), and (5.24). To fix ideas, suppose that all exogenous data are held constant except for the social rate of surplus value (e), which is subject to notional variations. Then, one can see that, although competition evens out profit and wage rates, their magnitudes are determined not from within competition but as functions of e (Liossatos 1980b). This is exactly what was lucidly proposed by Marx (1973):

> Competition among capitalists. . .may well even out, equalize the level of profit, but in no way creates the measure of this level. Likewise, competition among the workers could press down higher wages level, etc., but the general standard of wages. . .could not be explained by

> the competition between worker and worker, but only by the original relation between capital and labor. Competition generally, this essential locomotive force of the bourgeois economy, does not establish its laws, but is rather their executor (p. 552).

It can also be shown that the prices of iron (p_i) and corn (p_c) can be obtained through a transformation of values λ_i and λ_i, determined by the system of equations (5.14) and (5.15).

In conclusion, the transformation of value categories to their monetary expressions is a synchronic movement[9] from the abstract to the concrete – from the level of capital in general versus labor in general to that of competition. This transformation is not a movement from the immediate process of production to that of exchange, the latter becoming a derivative of the former. Accordingly, there is no notion of objective valuation that is defined by technology independently of exchange. The capitalist process is grasped at all levels of abstraction as an indissoluble unity of production and exchange. Thus, although the transformation does establish the primacy of the capital relation, the latter is a relation of production and a relation of exchange. This is why labor power is not a commodity like any other.

As an important corollary of the preceding propositions, we infer that there is no basis for either directly connecting labor values with exchange ratios or interpreting these values as just prices that define equivalent exchange. The prices of reproduction are what define equivalence in exchange.

The Question of Unequal Interregional Relations

As previously stated, many political economists consider the transformation of values to prices as an instance of unequal exchange. As a result of the equalization of the rate of profit across all branches of production, the mass of surplus value is unevenly distributed in favor of the sectors with a high value composition of capital at the expense of low-composition sectors. This inequality among sectoral capitals is expressed by the deviation of prices from respective values: sectors that sell their product above value gain at the expense of those selling below value.

As argued in the preceding section, the exchange of commodities at their equilibrium prices (of reproduction) is an exchange of equivalents; unequal exchange is inconceivable. Hence, the issue here is not merely to derive a more accurate criterion of regional unevenness by correcting Marx's solution to the transformation problem; instead, the question of regional inequalities must be placed on an entirely new basis.

It is instructive to begin with the price equations (5.3) and (5.4) and to ignore value for a moment. Actually, we need only the income identities in equations (5.9) through (5.11), which have been derived from the price equations. Let $k_i = K_i/L_i$, $k_c = K_c/L_c$, and $k = K/L$ denote capital intensities in the iron region, the corn region, and the economy as a whole, respectively. Then we can easily derive from equations (5.9) through (5.11) two relations linking per capita income to capital-intensity differentials; that is,

$$\frac{Y_i}{L_i} - \frac{Y}{L} = r(k_i - k) \qquad (5.25)$$

and

$$\frac{Y_c}{L_c} - \frac{Y}{L} = r(k_c - k) \qquad (5.26)$$

Thus, in a situation of simple reproduction under conditions of full competition (uniform profit and wage rates), regional disparities in per capita income exist if the degree of mechanization is not the same in all regions (nonuniform capital intensities). Suppose, for example, that the iron region is more capital-intensive than the corn region; that is, $k_i > k > k_c$. Then the iron region realizes a higher per capita income and the corn region a lower one than the national average (Y/L).

Parenthetically, it is intuitively obvious that our discussion is generalizable to any number of regions and commodities, including transportation costs. In this case, we would have one regional income identity for each region – such as equations (5.9) or (5.10) – and one national income identity. A per capita income relation such as equation (5.25) or (5.26) could be written for each and every region, the relevant capital intensities being regional averages.

Without the recognition of a higher level of abstraction – the level of value and surplus value in which the capital relation is expressed – one can hardly see any inequality behind the income disparities as depicted in equations (5.25) and (5.26). In fact, these disparities portray conditions of full equality within each social class. Capitalists and workers are rewarded in proportion to capital invested and labor performed, respectively. If, for instance, $k_i > k$, the iron region realizes a per capita income that is higher than the national average, simply because (1) capitalists in the iron region advance more capital – and hence realize more profit – per hour worked than the economy average, and (2) one hour of work earns the same payment everywhere in the economy. In fact, it is easy to see that disparities in per capita income are synonymous to disparities in per capita profits, because of the uniformity of the wage rate; that is, equations (5.25) and (5.26), respectively, yield

$$\frac{P_i}{L_i} - \frac{P}{L} = r(k_i - k) \qquad (5.27)$$

and

$$\frac{P_c}{L_c}-\frac{P}{L}=r(k_c-k) \tag{5.28}$$

where $P_i=rK_i$ and $P_c=rK_c$ denote profits in the iron and corn regions.

In sum, the price equations (5.3) and (5.4) do imply interregional income and profit disparities; but there is no way of inferring from the price equations alone that the relatively high per capita income of a given region is a gain at the expense of other regions. To investigate such a possibility, we must take into account the constraints in equations (5.23) and (5.24), which embed the price system in the space of value and surplus value.

Consider, first, the implication of the monetary constraint given in equation (5.24) or equation (5.17), which expresses the unity of the substance of value (abstract labor) and its monetary form. In view of equation (5.17), equations (5.25) and (5.26) become, respectively,

$$Y_i-mL_i=rL_i(k_i-k) \tag{5.29}$$

and

$$Y_c-mL_c=rL_c(k_c-k) \tag{5.30}$$

To interpret equations (5.29) and (5.30), one must recall that social production creates annually not only a physical net product (x_c) but also value L, which is the substance of society's purchasing power Y (national income) over the net product. Since the iron region, for example, creates value L_i per year, its contribution to the purchasing power of the society (national income) is the monetary expression mL_i. If, for example, $k_i>k$, then equation (5.29) implies that $Y_i>mL_i$ – that is, the iron region's command over the net product (regional income Y_i) is greater than its contribution to society's purchasing power. Since $Y_i+Y_c=mL_i+mL_c$, this can only happen at the expense ($Y_c<mL_c$) of the corn region. The opposite will be true if the corn region happens to be more capital-intensive. More generally, if one region exhibits more than average mechanization within a multiregion society, this region gains through exchange at the expense of one or more other regions.

Accordingly, regional disparities in per capita income do reflect unequal or assymetrical relations among regions. Such an inequality has nothing to do with unequal exchange, however. It is the effect of equivalent exchange, determined by prices of reproduction that are associated with fully competitive conditions.

A situation of equality would require that all regions realize incomes that equal the monetary expressions of their respective contributions to the value of the net product. In the presence of capital-intensity differentials, such a situation is impossible under conditions of full competition. When full competition prevails, the exchange of equivalents induces a redistribution of regional values and respective purchasing powers that amounts to a transfer of value (and hence of purchasing power) from the relatively low-capital-intensity regions to the relatively high-capital-intensity regions.

Consider, next, the additional effect of the constraint in equation (5.23), which expresses the determination of the distribution of income between wages and profits by the social rate of surplus value e (the balance of class forces). Apparently, regionally created values (L_i and L_c) can be decomposed into the value of labor power and surplus value – the regional counterparts of the decomposition in equation (5.18); that is, $L_i = V_i + S_i$ and $L_c = V_c + S_c$. If a uniform rate of exploitation (equal to e) in both regions is assumed, then the value of labor power in each region is transformed to regional wages in the same manner as in equation (5.20) – namely, $wL_i = mV_i$ and $wL_c = mV_c$. It is then easy to infer that equations (5.29) and (5.30) yield, respectively,

$$P_i - mS_i = rL_i(k_i - k) \tag{5.31}$$

and

$$P_c - mS_c = rL_c(k_c - k) \tag{5.32}$$

Equations (5.31) and (5.32) imply that value transfers from one region to another amount to surplus-value transfers – that is, unequal relations between regions amount to unequal relations between regionally-based fractions of capital. Capitalists in the corn region contribution a portion mS_c to the total profit ($P = mS$). If, for example, $k_c < k$, they realize profits (P_c) less than their contribution (mS_c) to the total profit. In view of equation (5.22), this can only happen because capitalists in the iron region gain ($P_i > mS_i$) at the expense of capitalists in the corn region.

What about value-price discrepancies? In the preceding case of surplus-value transfer from the corn to the iron region, we would expect, according to the traditional solution of the transformation problem, the price of corn to be less than its value ($p_c < m\lambda_c$); but this is not true. Because the net social product consists of only one commodity (corn), we see from equations (5.16) and (5.24) that $p_c = m\lambda_c$ – that is, corn is bought and sold at its labor value. Thus, the corn region may gain or lose surplus value (depending on capital intensities) without an associated inequality between value and price.

Nevertheless, we can still maintain the criterion of value-price inequalities if we compare relative values to relative prices. Thus, it can be shown that, if $p_i/p_c < \lambda_i/\lambda_c$, there is, in fact, a transfer of surplus value from the iron to the corn region, the opposite being true when $p_i/p_c > \lambda_i/\lambda_c$.

However, even this value-price comparison is not very helpful in a world of many regions and commodities. For example, if the corn region trades not only with the iron but also with another region specializing in the production of clothing, neither the sign of $p_c - m\lambda_c$ nor pair-wise comparisons of relative prices and values in isolation are sufficient to determine the sign of $Y_c - mL_c$; the latter depends in general on the sign and relative magnitude of the value-price difference for all commodities involved (Liossatos 1980a).

Furthermore, the traditional value-price criterion for value transfers cannot be applicable to the situations of incomplete regional specialization. For instance, if corn is produced in both regions of our hypothetical society under competitive conditions, then the deviation by the price from the value of corn does not indicate any value transfer. This is supposed to be one of the limitations of the theories of unequal exchange regarding international relations (De Janvry and Kramer 1979), given that the greatest volume of center-periphery trade involves nonspecific commodities (incomplete specialization). Accordingly, one could speak of interregional value transfers only under conditions of complete regional specialization.

Our results show that this is not true. Regardless of whether there is complete or incomplete specialization and whether transportation costs are significant or insignificant, one can always compare any given region's contribution to and realized share in the national income. This criterion pertains neither to a single value-price difference nor to a single, isolated act of exchange, but to the system of exchanges that link a given region to the rest of the world.

Concluding Remarks

The restructuring of the Sraffa system in the light of Marx's theory of value, surplus value, and money provides a theoretical framework for the analysis of unequal interregional relations. This restructuring has been effected by the grounding of Sraffian prices and distributive parameters on the capital relation. Thus, relations between things (prices and profit and wage rates) are captured as forms of relations between people – the social relations that characterize the capitalist mode of production. In this context, the transformation of value (abstract labor) into price categories is a synchronic movement from the level of the capital relation to the lower level of abstraction that pertains to the analysis of competition.

Further, we have argued that market exchange at equilibrium prices (of reproduction) is an exchange of equivalents – that is, no unequal exchange is conceivable at equilibrium prices. However, the reality to which erroneous conceptions of unequal exchange allude – transfers of economic value from less developed to more developed regions – can be captured in rigorous theoretical terms.

In fact, we have seen that the annual outcome of the process of social production is not only a physical net product but also value (society's overall annual labor), which is the substance of society's purchasing power (national income) over the net product. Hence, the contribution by any given region to national income can be defined and compared to the income actually realized in that region; this comparison tells us whether value has been transferred in net form or into the region. Thus, interregional value transfers are, in effect, transfers of purchasing power or command over the net social product. (The same holds true for transfers of surplus value.) Hence, statements concerning unequal interregional relations are positive theoretical deductions, which owe nothing to a normative comparison of the actual system with some ideal state of value-price equality.

The abolition of the rule of value-price inequality as a criterion of value and surplus-value transfers not only resolves a theoretical ambiguity but also allows us to remove the restrictive assumption of complete specialization in the analysis of unequal interregional relations. Our criteria for such relations are applicable to the situations of incomplete specialization and situations in which transportation costs are present. Accordingly, the theoretical setting developed in this chapter is promising for the analysis of interregional (and international) trade under these conditions.

Finally, it should be noted that, despite its theoretical focus and high level of abstraction, this chapter has suggested some interesting empirical explorations. The input-output framework provides a direct linkage with available data. Political economy variables, such as the rate of surplus value and the monetary expression of the working hour, can be estimated by methods suggested by Aglietta (1979). An empirical model, constructed along the theoretical lines of this chapter, would reveal the structure of interregional relations within a national economy and the extent of losses and gains in purchasing power in individual regions. It would also be possible to identify the relative significance of various differentials (differential capital-intensities, differential regional composition of labor, and so on) in interregional transfers of value.

Notes

1. For an excellent review and critique of theories of unequal exchange (in the context of international trade) see De Janvry and Kramer (1979).

2. Loosely defined, the transformation problem is the problem of translating value concepts (expressed in terms of abstract labor) such as the values of individual commodities, the rate of surplus value, and so on, to monetary magnitudes such as the prices of commodities, the rate of profit, and so on. The transformation problem has been discussed extensively in the literature. (Medio 1972; Morishima 1973; Morishima and Catephores 1978; Nuti 1977; Seton 1957; Shaikh 1977). See, also, Fine and Harris (1979) for a critical review of recent debates and more references. Whatever their merits – and there are many – existing conceptions and solutions of the transformation problem are inadequate from the standpoint of uncovering sectoral and regional inequalities beneath the equality of the market and full competition. As discussed later, the unity of the substance and monetary form of value is indispensable for such a task.

3. See Benetti (1974).

4. As we focus on the discussion of value, it is often convenient, but imprecise, to use the terms *commodity* and *value* interchangeably. We should always remember that a commodity is the unity of value and use-value.

5. See Sekine (1980) for an illuminating discussion of Marx's theory of value.

6. Thus, for example, "the direct intervention of money in the exchange process has been correctly absent from the analysis of the transformation" (Fine and Harris 1979, p. 33). Likewise, Seton (1957) sees no objective basis for choosing any particular invariance postulate in preference to all others; hence, he concludes that only relative prices can be linked to values.

7. In our discussion of the monetary form of value and related themes we draw upon the work of Aglietta (1979), particularly chapters 1 and 6.

8. See, for example, Levine (1978) and Sekine (1980) on this point.

9. The question of an alternative historical interpretation of the transformation problem is beyond the scope of this chapter. For some recent debates on this issue, see Catephores (1980) and Fine (1980).

References

Aglietta, Michel. 1979. *A Theory of Capitalist Regulation*. London: New Left Books.

Benetti, Carlo. 1974. *Valeur et Repartition*. Paris: Maspero.

Catephores, George. 1980. "The Historical Transformation Problem – A Reply." *Economy and Society* 9: 332–336.

De Janvry, Alain, and Kramer, Frank. 1979. "The Limits of Unequal Exchange." *Review of Radical Political Economics* 11 (Winter): 16–32.

Emmanuel, Arghiri. 1972. *Unequal Exchange: A Study of the Imperialism of Trade*. New York: Monthly Review Press.

Fine, Ben. 1980. "On the Historical Transformation Problem." *Economy and Society* 9: 337–339.

Fine, Ben, and Harris, Donald L. 1979. *Rereading Capital*. New York: Columbia University Press.

Harris, David J. 1978. *Capital Accumulation and Income Distribution*. Stanford: Stanford University Press.

Hunt, E. K., and Schwartz, J. G., Eds. 1972. *A Critique of Economic Theory*. Middlesex, England: Penguin.

Levine, David P. 1978. *Economic Theory*, vol. 1. London: Routledge and Kegan Paul.

Liossatos, Panagis. 1980a. "Unequal Exchange and Regional Disparities." *Papers of the Regional Science Association* 45: 87–103.

______. 1980b. "Surplus Value, Capitalist Competition and the Intersectoral Distribution of Monetary Income." Mimeographed. Philadelphia: University of Pennsylvania.

Marx, Karl. 1977. *Capital*, vol. 1. New York: Vintage.

______. 1967. *Capital*, vol. 3. New York: International Publishers.

______. 1973. *Grundrisse*. New York: Vintage Books.

Massey, Doreen. 1978. "Regionalism: Some Current Issues." *Capital and Class* 6: 106–125.

Medio, Alfredo. 1972. "Profits and Surplus Value: Appearance and Reality in Capitalist Production." In *A Critique of Economic Theory*, edited by E. K. Hunt and J. G. Schwartz, pp. 312–346.

Morishima, Michio. 1973. *Marx's Economics*. Cambridge, England: Cambridge University Press.

Morishima, Michio, and Catephores, George. 1978. *Value, Exploitation and Growth*. London: McGraw-Hill.

Nuti, Domenico Mario. 1977. "The Transformation of Labour Values into Production Prices and the Marxian Theory of Exploitation." In *The Subtle Anatomy of Capitalism*, edited by Jesse Schwartz, pp. 88–105.

Roemer, John E. 1978. "Marxian Models of Reproduction and Accumulation." *Cambridge Journal of Economics* 2: 27–53.

Schwartz, Jesse, Ed. 1977. *The Subtle Anatomy of Capitalism*. Santa Monica: Goodyear.

Sekine, Thomas T. 1980. "The Necessity of the Law of Value." *Science and Society* 45: 289–304.

Seton, F. 1957. "The 'Transformation Problem.' " *Review of Economic Studies* 24: 149–160.

Shaikh, Anwar. 1977. "Marx's Theory of Value and the 'Transformation Problem.' " In *The Subtle Anatomy of Capitalism,* edited by Jesse Schwartz, pp. 106–139.

Sraffa, Piero. 1960. *Production of Commodities By Means of Commodities.* Cambridge, England: Cambridge University Press.

II APPLICATIONS TO DEVELOPING COUNTRIES

6 MODE OF PRODUCTION AND SPATIAL ORGANIZATION IN PERU

Patricia Wilson Salinas

Peru epitomizes urban primacy: one single metropolitan area on the coast monopolizes the political, economic, and cultural life of the entire country.[1] Schematically, a regional scientist could say that Peru's spatial structure consists of a space dominated by Lima and the coast, with principal transport routes leading from the mining centers of the impoverished, underdeveloped *sierra* to the coast and to Lima. What was Peru's spatial structure like in the early sixteenth century, however, before the arrival of the Spaniards? The main axis of political, economic, and cultural life was the *sierra,* with the central hub at Cuzco. Peoples of the coast were politically dominated and economically exploited by those of the *sierra.* How did this radical switch occur, from *sierra* domination and coastal subservience to coastal dominance and *sierra* underdevelopment?

To answer this question requires a historical analysis spanning three modes of production. Because regional science explains spatial structure largely in terms of competitive (capitalist) market criteria, that approach is inadequate to the task. Instead, I use the tools and concepts of regional political economy described in chapter 1 in order to understand the logic of the different social systems and their spatial manifestations.

Pre-Incan Society

In fourteenth-century Peru, before the rise of the Incan empire, the principal motivating force of humankind was the struggle against nature to survive and reproduce. People organized into tribal villages, called *ayllus,* located in scattered, isolated areas throughout the harsh *sierra* and dry coast – wherever their artisanal, agricultural technology would permit. Since very little surplus could be generated with this technology, an egalitarian system of social relations was necessary, based on communal ownership of the means of production – land and tools. The division of labor was based on age and sex in a system of reciprocal aid among the villagers in differing productive tasks. The small surplus went to the village chief, who used most of it for the maintenance of a simple military, religious, and cultural superstructure (armaments, tombs, local divinities, and festivals). Social and economic inequality between chiefs and commoners was not great (Godelier 1974). In sum, the spatial organization of Peru in the fourteenth century clearly reflected the struggle between humans and nature as resolved in the mode of production based on the *ayllu*.

The Incan Empire

In the fourteenth century, one particular tribe was able to develop its productive forces sufficiently – largely through the improvement of potatoes and other tubers – to produce a surplus capable of maintaining a strong military and religious superstructure compared to that of the other tribes of the area. This tribe was the Incas, located in the village of Cuzco in the southern *sierra.* The Inca chiefs used the force of military coercion and religious persuasion to appropriate the agricultural surplus of the surrounding weaker *ayllus.* With this base, the Incan empire spread by the middle of the fifteenth century to the entire *sierra* and coast of what is now Peru and to parts of Bolivia, Chile, and Ecuador. The development of the Incan empire can be understood in light of the three basic motivating needs of the Incan chieftain class: (1) to maintain control over the conquered territories, (2) to increase the available surplus through the development of the productive forces throughout the empire, and (3) to channel that surplus to Cuzco.

The first task was accomplished, in part, by the manner of interfacing the Incan mode of production with the existing mode in the conquered territories. Maurice Godelier (1974) describes how that articulation reduced the chances of rebellion:

> Once these [ayllu] communities came under the domination of the Inca state they, or at least the ethnic and tribal groups which were organized in communities of this type, were profoundly modified. One part of their lands was expropriated and became the property of the [Incan] state or church. The communities also lost a part of their previous communal rights over the lands which they did retain, since the Inca state now claimed ultimate ownership over all the lands of the kingdom. In other words, the communities lost their control over the use

> of these lands and therefore forfeited their previous autonomy. Of the lands which remained in their hands, the usufruct rights remained the same as before the Inca conquest and production was still communally based. Nevertheless a new mode of production had been instituted . . . . [Yet] the previous forms of economic reciprocity and the ideology and ritual which corresponded to them [were retained, and] now served to the functioning of direct relations of exploitation and economic servitude, characteristic of the [new] mode. . . . To the extent that exploiters and exploited shared this same ideology [of politico-economic reciprocity and of religious representation], the oppression is *concealed* from both and is thus fully justified in the eyes of the first, and passively suffered, if not fully accepted, by the second. (pp. 64–65, 71)

Another strategy for securing the conquered *ayllus* was territorial integration through a system of cities, roads, and regional administration. Such integration also served the important purpose of channeling surplus back to Cuzco, the political, military, and religious capital of the empire.

The most important physical infrastructure for territorial integration was the system of stone paths, whose main axis followed the entire *sierra* of Peru and stretched into Ecuador and Chile. Two principal branches were constructed as well: one to the coast at Pachacamac, near Lima, and the other to Chan Chan, near Trujillo (see figure 6-1).

The system of secondary cities (subordinate to Cuzco) was built in the areas to the north to facilitate the long, difficult conquest of the relatively advanced *ayllus* found there, to maintain control over them after the conquest, and to channel agricultural surplus from them back to Cuzco. Jauja was built in the central *sierra* at the junction with the road to Pachacamac, as a center of operations during the conquest and control of the tribes on the central coast. Cajamarca, in the northern *sierra,* began as a center for the conquest of the tribes to the north. Chan Chan, on the north coast, was established as the center of control over the conquered coastal tribes of Mochica and Chavin. The *ayllus* of the southern *sierra* could be controlled directly from Cuzco, and no subordinate city was established.

The Incas established a regional administrative structure in which every ten *ayllus* were coordinated into a *chunca,* under an authority recognized by and responsible to the Incan state in Cuzco. As the empire expanded, the *chuncas* were organized into large regional bodies, called *suyus.* There were four *suyus,* each dominated by one of the four major cities and each connected to Cuzco by the system of paved paths (Caceres et al. 1973).

To increase available agriculture surplus in the empire, the Incas developed their primitive technology to the fullest. They designed efficient irrigation systems and installed them largely in the early conquered lands in the southern *sierra* near Cuzco. This infrastructure increased labor productivity and cultivable land area, resulting in a greater surplus going to the military storehouses in Cuzco.

The logic behind the early spatial formation of Peru lay in the creation of a

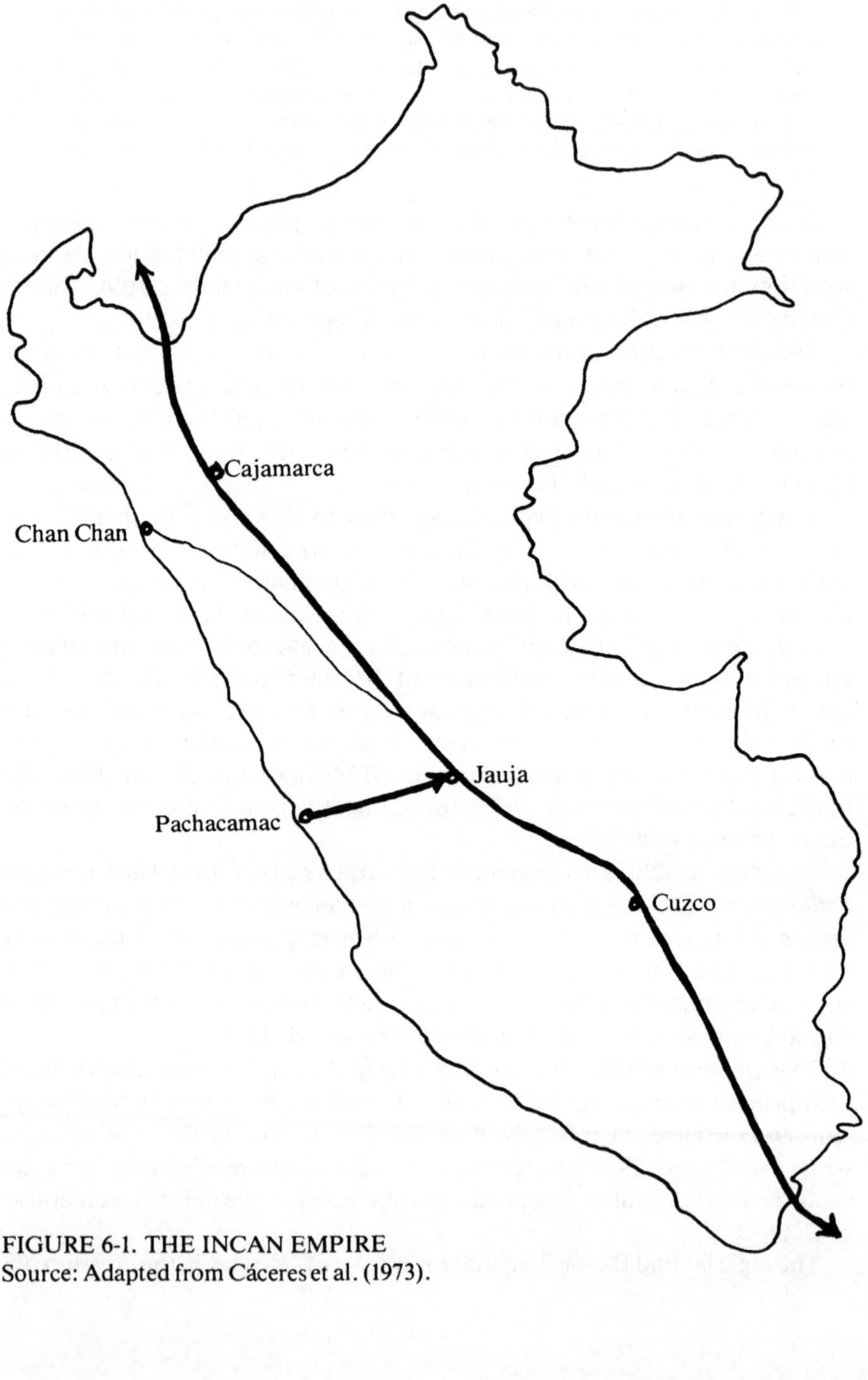

FIGURE 6-1. THE INCAN EMPIRE
Source: Adapted from Cáceres et al. (1973).

sierra-based system of cities and transport routes designed not to produce surplus but to appropriate it from the conquered *ayllus* and channel it to the imperial capital of Cuzco in the Andes.

Early Mercantilist Period

The Europeans, with their technologically more advanced feudal mode of production, entered Latin America in the sixteenth century, during the rise of mercantilist trading, to look for marketable surplus. The military and missionary expeditions' most important objective was to establish in the Americas a mode of production capable of producing a surplus that could be appropriated by the European metropolis and sold quickly in the European markets. To this end, it was necessary to modify the productive relations where possible or to introduce new ones where necessary in order to assure (1) the production of value greater than that necessary for the subsistence of the direct producers (that is, the production of a surplus) and (2) the production of a surplus in the form of goods demanded for use in the European market (Singer and Cardoso 1972, pp. 5–6).

The productive system in the Incan empire of the early sixteenth century already was producing a significant agricultural surplus,[2] but there was no market in Europe for that kind of surplus. The European feudal communities were self-sufficient in basic food items, and the landlords sold their surplus to the fledgling cities of Europe to buy the luxury goods produced by the urban artisans and imported from the Orient by the merchants. The principal market in Europe for consumer goods was in luxury goods, because of the incredible concentration of surplus in the hands of the feudal aristocracy. European artisanal production for the luxury market was protected by mercantilist laws against external competition, and Peruvian artisanry could not compete with the silks, cotton cloth, jewelry, fine furniture, porcelain, and tapestries from the Orient, where the social formations had produced a highly developed artisanal production of luxury goods for the local aristocracy. The only other potential form of marketable surplus was gold and silver, which were already used as a basis for exchange in the expanding mercantilist trade of Europe. Gold and silver could be exchanged immediately for any other article on the European market; so, to insert Latin America into an international division of labor based on the needs of the dominant European mode of production, the conquerers — specifically, the Spanish — searched for gold and silver as they took over the American lands. The Spaniards found the greatest sources of gold and silver in Mexico and Peru (Singer and Cardoso 1972, pp. 7–9).

How did the European mercantilist, feudal mode of production from Europe interact with the weaker mode in Peru? Since there was no existing productive organization for metal extraction, the Spanish developed a system of forced labor called the *mita,* in which peasants were obligated to do the grueling work of the mines with primitive technologies. The Spaniards used the indigenous agriculture production to provide the means of subsistence for the mine workers. Since the Incan mode was already efficiently producing agricultural surplus and channeling it to the Incan state in Cuzco, the Spaniards tried to take advantage of the existing productive structure. They conserved its collective form but replaced the surplus appropriators – the Incan state – with their own representatives, the *encomenderos,* in a new form called the *encomienda.* Simultaneously, the Incan priests were replaced by Christian priests, who ideologically legitimized the exploitation of the Indians. Although the former *ayllus* continued to be worked communally, the land was owned by the individual Spanish *encomenderos,* who extracted surplus in the form of crops, much in the manner of feudal Europe, and channeled sufficient surplus to the export mining sector to maintain the indentured workers. In this manner, the colonizing Spaniards reorganized a system that permitted the simultaneous exploitation of the forced labor in the export mining sector and the peasants that remained in the internal-subsistence agriculture sector. The result was a sizable surplus of gold and silver bullion for the royal coffers of the mother country.

The next problem facing the colonizers was to channel the new mineral surplus safely and efficiently back to the Spanish Crown. To do so, they reinforced the Incan road system, particularly in the southern *sierra,* where the major mineral deposits were found (near Ayacucho, Arequipa, and Potosi), in order to bring the precious metals from the *sierra* to the coast. The coastal cities established by the Spaniards for purposes of conquest and control (Lima, Trujillo, Lambayeque, and Tumbes) were given the new, very important function of serving as transshipment intermediaries to the Spanish metropolis (see figure 6-2). Some of the surplus stayed in the colonial cities to support the soldiers, functionaries, priests, and merchants, but most of it was appropriated by the Crown.

Transferring surplus to the metropolis was not a peaceful process. The threat from smugglers, pirates, and rival colonialists required vast military protection. To reduce this threat, most of the surplus from throughout Peru was brought together for transshipment at one principal point, Lima, which was located at the maritime terminal of the Incan road to the mineral-rich southern *sierra.* Chosen as the capital, Lima became the principal link with the metropolis, not only as an intermediary for mineral surplus but also because of its administrative functions.

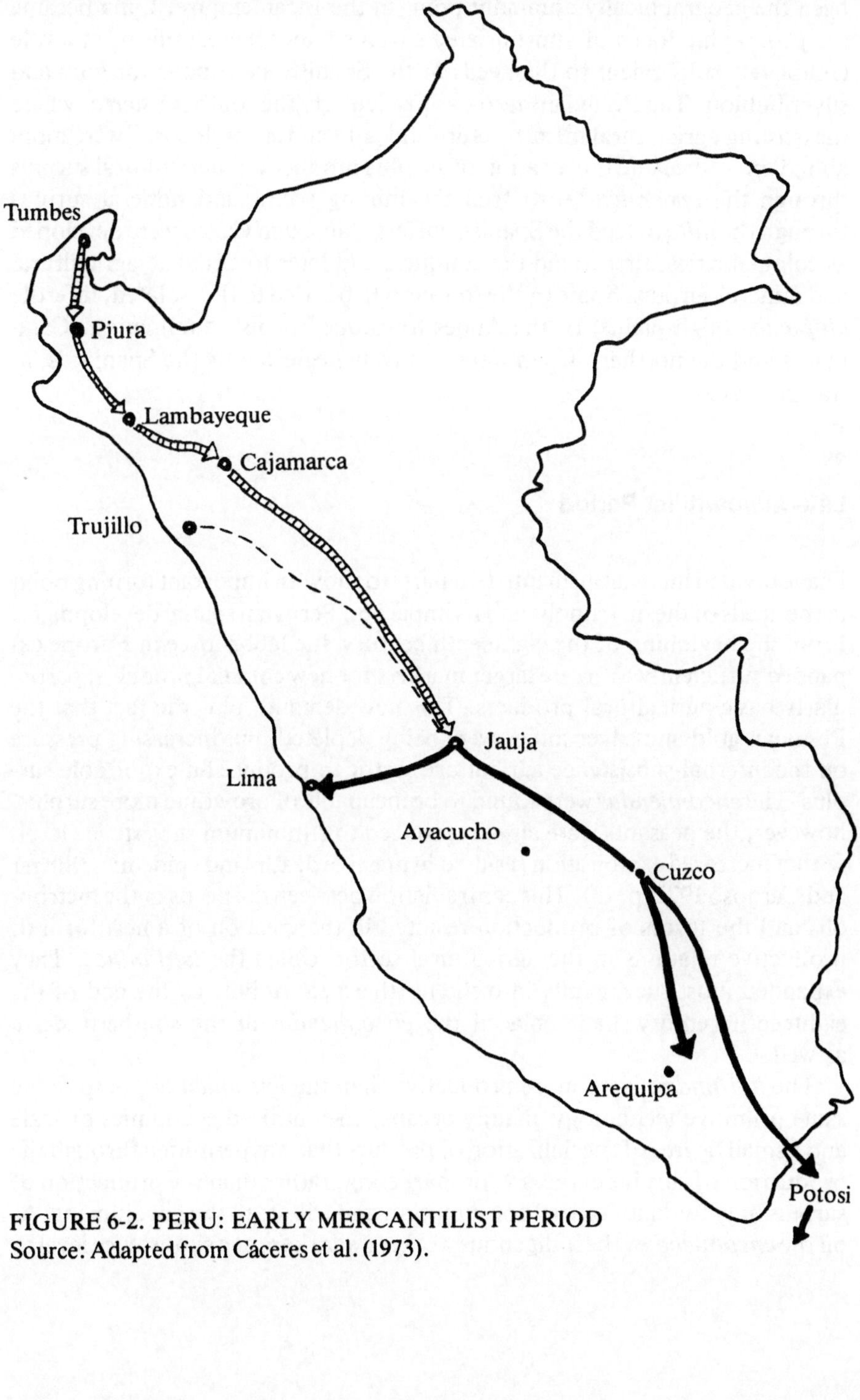

FIGURE 6-2. PERU: EARLY MERCANTILIST PERIOD
Source: Adapted from Cáceres et al. (1973).

Spatial organization in Peru in the sixteenth, seventeenth, and eighteenth centuries clearly reflected the needs of mercantile Spain. Whereas Cuzco had been the geographically dominant point in the Incan empire, Lima became the geographic focus of appropriated surplus under mercantilism, in a role completely subservient to the needs of the Spanish metropolis for gold and silver bullion. The Peruvian *sierra* – particularly the southern *sierra,* where the existing agricultural infrastructure and gold and silver deposits were more abundant – became the location of surplus production: agricultural surplus through the *encomiendas* to feed the mining sector and mineral surplus through the *mita* to feed the Spanish coffers. Jauja and Cuzco were developed as colonial cities, first to aid the conquest and later to circulate agricultural and mineral surplus. Some of the southern tribes fled to the isolated, infertile *altiplanos* (high plains) of the Andes to escape Spanish domination. Cajamarca and the northern *sierra* were relatively neglected by the Spaniards, as was the *selva.*

Late Mercantilist Period

I have divided mercantilism into two parts to show an important turning point in the needs of the metropolis and its impact on Peruvian spatial development. From the beginning of the eighteenth century, the labor force in Europe expanded sufficiently to create larger markets for new colonial products, particularly basic agricultural products. This new demand, plus the fact that the Peruvian gold and silver mines were being depleted, put increasing pressure on the internal-subsistence agriculture sector to produce an exportable surplus. The *encomiendas* were found to be incapable of providing more surplus, however; the peasants were already reduced to a minimum subsistence level, so that increased exploitation resulted in massive deaths and epidemics (Singer and Cardoso 1972, p. 13). This contradiction between the needs of the metropolis and the forces of production resulted in the creation of a new form of productive relations in the agricultural sector, called the *latifundios.* They expanded most successfully into the northern *sierra* but, by the end of the eighteenth century, had replaced the *encomiendas* in the southern *sierra* as well.

The *latifundios* were more productive than the *encomiendas,* despite the same primitive technology, mainly because they utilized economies of scale and a small degree of specialization of product that was permitted through the production of surplus expressly for marketing, rather than the production of surplus only for landholders' consumption and tribute to the government. As on the *encomiendas,* the indigenous workers were kept at a subsistence level to maximize the appropriable surplus. Even though they were "free" tenants, their debts to the *latifundistas* enslaved them to the land. The *latifundista* purchased his land from the Crown, unlike the *encomendero,* whose position always depended on the royal favor.[3] By the end of the eighteenth century, the forces of production on the *latifundios* were sufficiently developed to allow a regular exportable surplus.

The commercial function of the coastal cities grew rapidly in importance as a result of the new agricultural surplus. Although Lima was the principal beneficiary of the new surplus, other cities, such as Trujillo, Lambayeque-Chiclayo, and Piura, also stepped up their commercial activities (see figure 6-3). Not only did the cities export the surplus directly to the Spanish metropolis, they also shipped the growing regional agricultural specialties between regions of Peru, using the coastal axis as the main channel of internal commerce.

One of the important consequences of the expanding commercial functions of the coastal cities was the development of a new class of merchants, financiers (usurers), and transporters. Some of the cities – particularly Lima, but also Trujillo, Lambayeque-Chiclayo, and Piura – grew richer; and, as they did, they attracted more and more of the rural elite to the residential comforts and glitter of urban life. As a result, the urban service sector mushroomed. The cities – especially Lima – became the focal point of the cultural and political life of the colony and a center of increased demand for imported luxury goods from Europe. By the end of the eighteenth century, Spain recognized its American colonies not only as a source of monetary metals but also as a market for European goods. Despite this urban market, Peru was still a rural country; almost the entire population (90 percent) lived in the rural areas, and nearly all the economic surplus was produced there (see table 6-1).

The economic, political, and cultural growth of the colonial cities harbored the collapse of colonial life itself – the movement for independence, led by the colonial mercantilists and supported by the *latifundistas,* who wanted more control over Peru's surplus. Because of the growing hegemony of English-dominated industrial capitalism over mercantilism, the Spanish could not prevent the declaration of Peruvian independence in 1821 and the substitution of English for Spanish hegemony over Peru.

The implications of late mercantilism for the urban development along Peru's coast are clear: growth of the *latifundio* system in the *sierra* to increase agricultural surplus for export; increasing commercial importance of the coastal cities for exporting the agricultural surplus and importing luxury goods for the growing *criolla* elite; reinforcement of the coastal axis for internal trade; and transformation of some of the coastal cities – with Lima at their head – into the colonial cultural and political centers for the Peruvian upper class and the breeding place of the independence movement.

FIGURE 6-3. PERU: LATE MERCANTILIST PERIOD
Source: Adapted from Cáceres et al. (1973).

Table 6-1. The Population of Peru and Selected Cities, 1750–1923 *(in thousands)*

Year	*Peru*	*Lima*	*Callao*	*Cuzco*	*Arequipa*	*Trujillo*	*Ayacucho*	*Chiclayo*
1754	984	54 (1755)		26 (1750)				
1791	1,077	53		32	24	6	26	
1812		64						
1836	1,374	56						
1850	2,001							
1862	2,488	89	18	24	22	8	20	9
1876	2,699	100	34	20	29	8	10	11
1908	3,548	155	33 (1905)				14	
1920	4,376	203	52	33	44 (1917)	22	15	16 (1923)

Source: Adapted from Richard M. Morse, p. 416.

Industrial Capitalism

The change from feudalism to industrial capitalism, and the concomitant change from Spanish domination to English domination, brought with it no major alteration in Peru's internal productive structure or social relations. Peru retained its colonial mercantilist functions of channeling agricultural and mineral surplus to the metropolis (now English) through the commercial and financial intermediation of Lima and other coastal cities. The English bourgeoisie's needs for an increasing number of raw materials, because of the industrial revolution, caused Peru to diversify its exports – adding, first, guano and nitrates and, after the 1870s, cotton and sugar from the new coastal plantations – but without changing its role of raw material exporter and luxury good importer. This diversification integrated Peru more deeply into the European economy, making the new nation liable to the vicissitudes of European demand and business cycles. While European capitalism flourished, Peru remained in precapitalist modes of production, since the dominant mode needed only the diversification of exportable production and a greater monetarization of the Peruvian economy.

Class relations between appropriators and producers in Peru did not change significantly. The peasant remained at a level of subsistence as the *sierra latifundios* completely replaced the *encomiendas* and the last Spanish masters were supplanted by national *criollos*. For the appropriators – the Peruvian financial, commercial, and landed oligarchy – independence meant that a larger amount of surplus – what before had gone to Spain in tributes – stayed in Peru. Through national taxation, some of the surplus helped to build a national urban bureaucracy. Some of it helped the balance of payments and increased the capacity to import, thus favoring the merchants and financiers. The incipient class of urban artisans (the petite bourgeoisie), favored by the restricted capacity to import during the colonial period, was destroyed by Peru's further dependence on the European economy for imported consumer goods.

Spatial organization during the English domination was largely a continuation of colonial trends: further growth of the cities and the coastal axis, reinforced by the rapid expansion of the state bureaucracy in Lima, the growth of high-productivity plantation agriculture on the north coast,[4] and the appearance of coastal boom towns because of the rapidly expanding guano market; the growing urban domination of the country by extracting surplus through taxes, commercial intermediation, and land rent, just as during colonial times; and diversification of mineral exports and building of railroads and highways from the coast to new mineral sources (particularly in the northern *sierra,* such as Ancash). The only major new element in Peru's spatial organization during the English domination was the development of Iquitos, the Amazon port in the Peruvian *selva,* as an important trade link with the Atlantic. The development of Iquitos reflected the general decline of Lima's importance to the European metropolis and the comparative rise of the Atlantic seaboard countries and Chile as the most conveniently located providers of raw materials for the English metropolis (see figure 6-4).[5]

Monopoly Capitalism

At the turn of the century, England's dominance and competitive industrial capitalism gave way to U.S. dominance and monopoly capitalism. The U.S. multinational corporations began investing directly in the extraction of Peru's minerals and plantation crops for export, thus reinforcing the development of extractive enclaves in the coast and the *sierra* and strengthening the financial and commercial (that is, nonproductive) roles of Lima and the other coastal cities.

The period of advanced monopoly capitalism began in Peru after World War II, when multinational corporations spearheaded the country's industrialization process. Advanced monopoly capitalism represented a new international division of labor, in which the foreign appropriators (largely U.S. multinational corporations) needed not only to continue extracting surplus in the form of mineral and agricultural products for export but also to use Peru as an additional market for their technology and capital goods. These needs translated spatially to (1) continuation of extractive enclaves (minerals in the *sierra,* plantation agriculture on the coast, and, later, oil in the *selva*), all with wage relations and advanced technology; and (2) urban-industrial growth along the coast, to create a market for manufactured goods and processed raw materials for export. The *sierra,* aside from the mineral enclaves, was needed only as a source of cheap wage goods (foodstuffs) to keep wages down in the industrial workforce. As a result, the 1950s and 1960s witnessed rapid urban growth and surplus accumulation in Lima and the coastal cities, and, in the *sierra,* continuation of labor-intensive technologies, largely nonwage relations, and price mechanisms favoring urban industrial products.

During advanced monopoly capitalism in Peru, the major agents affecting the process of spatial formation were the foreign bourgeoisie, with its control of technology, the Peruvian grand-export bourgeoisie in alliance with foreign capitalists, the middle bourgeoisie producing for the internal market, and the government. The bourgeoisie considered three main factors in location decisions: the availability of a sufficiently exploitable labor force, raw materials that the workers could transform into value, and markets for circulating the

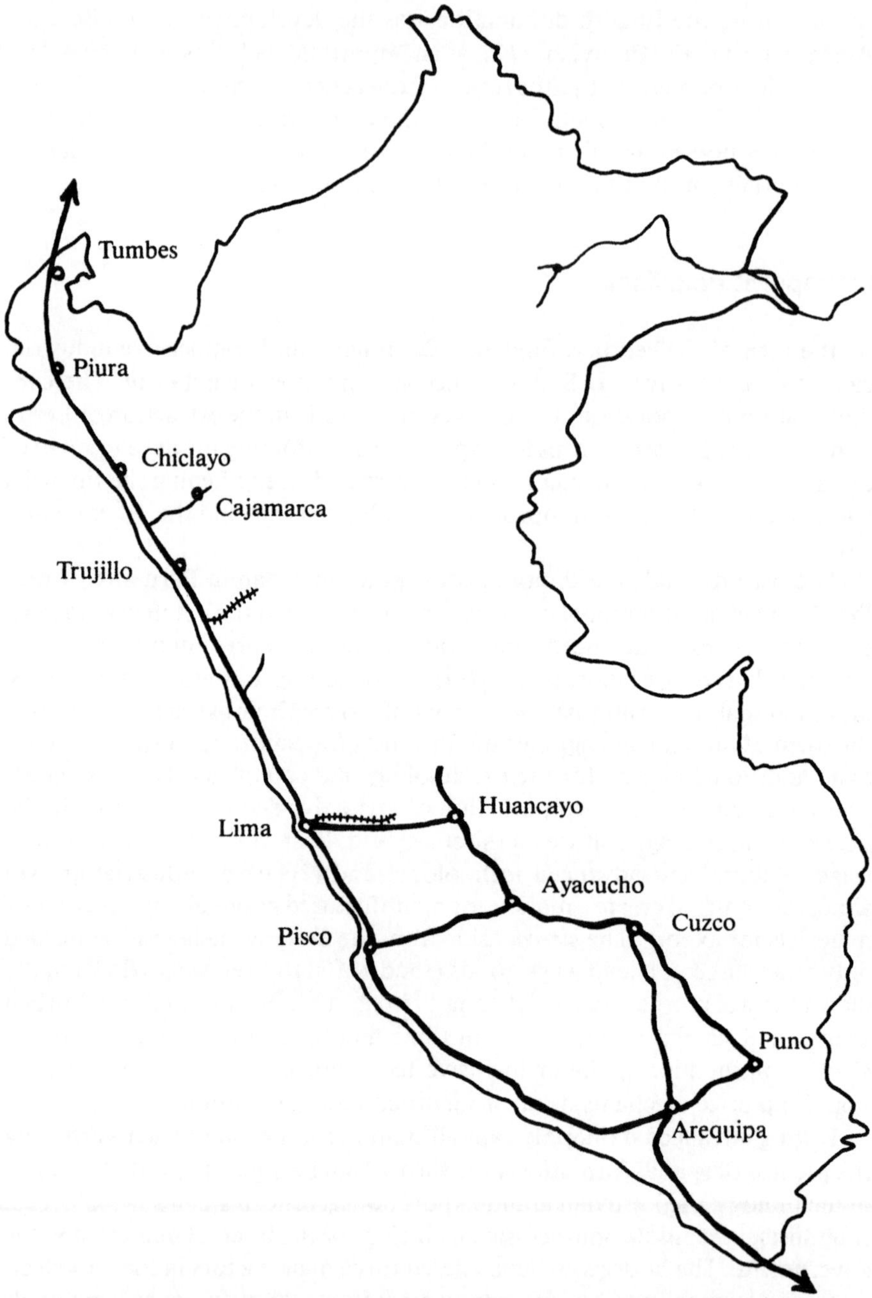

FIGURE 6-4. PERU: PERIOD OF INDUSTRIAL CAPITALISM
Source: Adapted from Cáceres et al. (1973).

surplus value and realizing a profit. However, the needs of each fraction of the bourgeoisie varied. Monopoly capitalists, both foreign and national, were less concerned about the preexistence of an exploitable labor force, since their capital-intensive technologies allowed them relative exploitation of labor (that is, surplus extraction from labor through increasing labor productivity rather than reducing real wages). Monopoly capitalists could usually attract the necessary labor force to any location. In fact, monopoly capitalists often preferred to locate outside large labor market areas (that is, metropolitan areas), where labor unrest was high. Proximity to raw materials was the most important factor for the export monopoly capitalists, who usually located their plants on the coast, nearest the source of the raw materials. An empirical analysis of provincial industrial location showed these largely foreign-controlled industrial enclaves along the coast (Salinas 1975).

Rapid circulation was an important factor for competitive industrial capitalists producing for the internal market. They generally located near Lima, where most of the high-income market was located. Found largely among the middle bourgeoisie producing for the internal market, competitive capitalists also frequently had to resort to absolute exploitation (reducing real wages to extract a larger surplus) because of their less-productive technology. Thus, competitive capitalists usually located in Lima not only for rapid circulation but for a larger labor force that permitted absolute exploitation.

The role of the public sector in influencing spatial organization in Peru was particularly interesting during the period of advanced monopoly capitalism. Concerted efforts were made, both by the Belaunde government in the 1960s and the military government in the early 1970s, to alter spatial organization in Peru. Since these governments ostensibly represented the interests of the middle industrial bourgeoisie and populist groups that wanted a significantly expanded internal market for final goods, they tried to redistribute income and wealth among social classes and regions. However, an impressive array of government programs designed to decentralize both spatially and socially the concentration of surplus in Lima and the coastal cities — for example, agrarian reform, investment incentives, public infrastructure construction — had little effect.[6] The state, as an arena of conflict among the various classes and class fractions, was responsive mainly to the strongest fractions: the foreign bourgeoisie and grand-export bourgeoisie. Thus, industrial enclave development continued, actually reinforced by many government actions (Salinas, 1975, 1977).

Conclusions

The utility of basic political economy concepts — for example, mode of production, surplus, class, superstructure, and conflict among classes and modes

– for understanding the logic behind the history of Peru's spatial organization should now be evident. Since the days of the Spanish conquest, Peru's integration into a dominant foreign mode of production – European feudalism and international capitalism – has been the primary force behind its changing spatial organization. A new phase of advanced monopoly capitalism, with a new international division of labor based on the integration of production on a world scale, is beginning to be felt in Peru now. Implying a potentially significant impact on the country's spatial organization, this new phase of development will provide another fruitful object of investigation, requiring the tools and concepts of regional political economy.

Notes

1. Metropolitan Lima has a population more than twenty times the size of the second largest city, produces nearly three-quarters of the country's manufacturing output, and concentrates over four-fifths of the nation's bank deposits. The remainder of Peru's industrial activity and urban population is found largely in a few cities along the coast. The Peruvian Andes (hereafter referred to as the *sierra*) have a large part of the population but are almost totally rural, with a per capita income only one-fifth that of Lima's (Webb 1972, p. 16). This subsistence income reflects the predominance of traditional, low-productivity agriculture with vast underemployment broken up only by a few highly productive enclaves of mineral extraction. The jungle area of Peru (hereafter referred to as the *selva*), comprising 57 percent of the land surface, is largely unpopulated and undeveloped except for the coffee and tobacco plantations and the Amazon free port of Iquitos.

2. In Brazil, where a surplus-producing mode of production was not found, the Portuguese had to set up new productive relations – namely, the sugar cane haciendas, using primarily imported slave labor (Singer and Cardoso 1972).

3. The *latifundio* is to be distinguished from the plantation, which was dedicated to one principal export crop and developed later, mainly in the northern coastal valleys.

4. Plantation agriculture (namely, large-scale production of sugar and cotton for export) developed on the north coast in the 1870s for two main reasons: (1) coastal labor shortage and the high cost of imported labor encouraged the coastal landowners to adopt more capital intensive technologies; and (2) metropolitan demand for sugar and cotton was large. The rise of coastal plantation agriculture sparked the growth of productivity differences with the traditional agriculture of the sierra (Favre 1971).

5. For an explanation of spatial formation in Latin America as a whole, see Quijano (1970).

6. For an empirical corroboration that quantifies the distribution of labor productivity and allocation of surplus over space and between social-class fractions in Peru, see Salinas (1975). The author also performs a regression analysis that indicates that differential labor productivity over space is more a function of the firm's relation to the foreign industrial enclave than of comparative regional advantages.

References

Cáceres, Juan, et al. 1973. *Metropolitizacion en America Latina: El Caso Peruano.* Lima: Universidad Nacional de Ingenieria, Instituto de Planeamiento de Lima.

Favre, Henri. 1971. "El Desarrollo y Las Formas del Poder Oligarquico en el Peru." In *La Oligarquia en el Peru,* 2nd ed., edited by Jose Matos Mar et al. Lima: Serie Peru Problema, No. 2, Instituto de Estudios Peruanos.

Frank, A.G. 1973. *Lumpenburguesia, Lumpen Desarrollo: Dependencia, Clase, y Politica en Latinoamerica.* Buenos Aires: Ediciones Periferia, S.R.L.

Godelier, Maurice. 1974. "On the Definition of a Social Formation: The Example of the Incas." *Critique of Anthropology* 1.

Instituto Nacional de Planificacion del Peru. 1974. *Indicadores Regionales.* Anexo 2. Lima.

Marx, Karl. 1859. *Contribution to the Critique of Political Economy.*

______. 1861. *Capital.*

Montoya Rojas, Rodrigo. 1970. *A Proposito del Caracter Predominantemente Capitalista de la Economia Peruana Actual.* Serie: Formacion Social y Estructura Economica, no. 1. Lima: Ediciones Teoria y Realidad.

Morales, Miguel, and Licio, Parisi. 1972. *Modo de Produccion, Proceso de Regionalizacion y Relaciones Cuidad-Campo.* Santiago: Instituto Latinoamericano de Planificacion Economica y Social.

Morse, Richard M. 1974. "Trends and Patterns of Latin American Urbanization, 1750–1920," *Comparative Studies in Society and History,* Vol. 16, No. 4.

Quijano, Anibal. 1970. "Dependencia, Cambio Social, y Urbanizacion en Latinoamerica." In *America Latina: Ensayos de Interpretacion Sociologico-Politica,* edited by F.H. Cardoso, Anibal Pinto, and Osvaldo Sunkel. Santiago: Editorial Universitaria.

Salinas, Patricia Wilson. 1974. "Influencias institucionales en el desequilibrio espacial del Peru: la regionalizacion de las inversiones publicas." Serie Documento de Trabajo, no. 21. Lima: CISEPA, Universidad Catolica.

______. 1975. *From Mode of Production to Spatial Formation: the Regional Consequences of Dependent Industrialization in Peru.* Ithaca: Cornell Dissertation Series in Planning.

______. 1977. "Le developpement regional et les limites d'une reforme: l'experience au Perou du gouvernement militaire." *Revue Tiers-Monde* 18: 723–736.

Singer, Paul Israel, and Cardoso, Fernando H. 1972. "A Cidade E.O. Campo." *Cadernos CEBRAP,* no. 7.

Webb, Richard, 1972. "The Distribution of Income in Peru." Princeton University, Discussion Paper No. 26.

7 THE INTERNATIONALIZATION OF CAPITAL AND THE SPATIAL ORGANIZATION OF AGRICULTURE IN MEXICO

David Barkin

The internationalization of capital is gradually transforming the economic structures of most countries participating in the world capitalist system. The process involves the integration of individual countries and their constituent regions into an increasingly unified whole, in which each unit is expected to contribute to the needs of the whole. With the resulting greater freedom for international investment and trade, the market is expected to allocate resources efficiently to ensure higher levels of economic activity and income. Economists postulate that, ideally, the internationalization of capital will lead to an effective national and regional integration based on comparative advantages, which will improve the welfare of all participants.

Reality is far removed from this idealized statement of neoclassical international trade theory. Although the internationalization of capital is occurring at an ever-accelerating pace, effectively integrating national and regional economies into a global whole, the welfare implications of this change are not all beneficial. Based on the experience of the modernization of the primary sector in Mexico, it is clear that, although the internationalization of capital offers real benefits to its trading partners, it imposes severe costs on the poor country as a whole and disproportionate hardships on the poorer regions and social classes in particular.

Mexican export promotion policies, like those of other countries, are particularly obvious examples of this process in operation. They were adopted after the realization of the failure of import-substituting industrialization (ISI) to promote self-sustained economic development. The resulting industries were inefficient and did not generate even the anticipated volume of employment. Furthermore, instead of easing the foreign exchange problem, the

ISI approach appeared to make it more intractable; the need for imports became embedded in the economic structure itself. It also resulted in increasing unemployment, inequality, and distorted economic structures. To solve these problems, a new stage of ISI was proposed to encompass intermediate goods and capital equipment manufacture while encouraging exports and subjecting the economy to international competition.

One result of this internationalization has been a revolution in Mexican agriculture. Formerly poor and technologically backward, the small but productive part of this sector can now boast of its modernity and its important contributions to Mexican export earnings up to 1980. Part of the revolutionary process, however, has left the vast majority of the nation's farmers (peasants) on subsistence and infrasubsistence plots, working with traditional methods and experiencing continuing impoverishment. This evolution has produced some very disturbing results, which are now the foci of national debate and concern: (1) the country has again become incapable of supplying itself with its own basic food requirements, even at the reduced levels of effective demand since the devaluation; (2) it does not even have the physical infrastructure to accommodate the increasing volumes of grains that must be imported to sustain actual levels of consumption; (3) it is faced with growing unemployment and disguised unemployment in the rural areas, which are increasingly serious problems because industrial development is also incapable of contributing to the solution of these employment problems; and (4) the agricultural sector no longer generates foreign exchange for capital accumulation in other sectors.

Although these problems are serious concerns of the present regime and present some real threats to the very stability of the nation's socioeconomic model, it appears that present economic policies are designed to accelerate recent structural tendencies. These policies promote greater competitiveness of agricultural production in the context of international markets and implicitly leave the traditional peasant producers to their own fortunes. The rhetorical concern afforded this group is translated into official programs explicitly designed to transform them into capitalist producers or proletarians, working lands to which they have little more than legal title. The process of transforming peasants into proletarians, however, has inherent limits. The changes in the structure of the Mexican economy threaten the sociopolitical integrity of peasant communities. Unlike other changes, which thrust untold millions of people into the ranks of proletarians or marginal groups in the urban areas, the agricultural transformation presents another possibility: with direct challenges to the prevailing order, the peasant communities may refuse to submit to their own systematic destruction.

This chapter specifically addresses the impacts on spatial organization — including, as defined in chapter 3, the relations of production — in Mexico's agricultural regions caused by the changing international division of labor. The impacts are addressed in terms of changes in (1) technology and product mix, (2) the agricultural work process and decision making, (3) vulnerability to international forces, and (4) agro-industrialization. First, however, the important role of public policy in facilitating the internationalization of capital in Mexico is traced.

The Role of Public Policy

The fundamental cause of the changes in the relations of production in Mexico's agriculture is the growing effectiveness of international economic forces to influence farm-level activity in Mexico. However, the transmission of international prices and the growing participation of direct foreign investment, industry, and foreign agricultural distributors in the primary producing sector have been directly facilitated by Mexican governmental policy to modernize agriculture. A brief review of the government's decision-making process may be instructive for a better understanding of the underlying mechanisms that determine the country's role in the international economy.

During the 1950s, intensive government-supported research into improved seeds for wheat and hybridization for corn (maize) produced new varieties that offered the possibility of greatly improved yields and the promise of agricultural self-sufficiency at much higher levels of per capita consumption in Mexico. Official policy was supportive of this effort, creating the physical infrastructure — large-scale irrigation projects — necessary to take advantage of the new productive potential.

The changes in the productive structure occasioned by this investment and innovation opened new horizons. The country could plan on self-sufficiency in grains while expanding production of some basic export products. Agriculture played its classical role in economic development: providing the foodstuffs and freeing labor for national growth while generating the foreign exchange needed to support industrial investment. It was clear to all who bothered to look, however, that this structure exacerbated substantial inequalities within the primary sector. Corn continued to be produced by peasants on the poorest lands, and wheat covered part of the modernized irrigation districts.

The government's original decision to emphasize the production of basic food production (wheat and corn) was consistent with economic policies in the early stage of development policy in Mexico. It is interesting that this was also consistent with the U.S. vision of the world economy at that time. Mexico had embarked on an effort to become increasingly self-sufficient in industrial and food production. The ISI program established in the 1950s was a perfect complement to the efforts to improve agricultural productivity by heavy investments in infrastructure; domestic production of grains proved to be the dynamic element in promoting a rapid rate of agricultural production. Concerned with its role as an industrial nation, the United States was preoccupied during this period with limiting its production of these basic food products, shipping its surpluses off to various parts of the world as food aid, which, ironically, weakened the domestic productive capability of many a recipient nation.

Agriculture at that time was not a particularly important target of foreign investment in Mexico. There were substantial foreign interests in cotton production but limited interests in sugar and other tropical products, for historical reasons. The 1917 land reform made direct foreign participation in agriculture difficult, as foreign land purchases were restricted and land rentals were nominally prohibited on land distributed to Mexicans. In this environment, Mexico was able to pursue its policy of national self-sufficiency and ISI without hostile pressures from abroad.

With the gradual realization of the growing foreign exchange problems created by ISI, the nation's policymakers were obliged to rethink their development strategies. As part of this process, a raging debate in economic theory was reproduced in the corridors of power – comparative advantages versus national self-sufficiency. Reduced to its most simple terms, the debate posed the question of whether the nation could afford to dedicate its most productive resources to producing goods for domestic consumption rather than for export. The arguments for a shift to the criterion of comparative advantages, firmly grounded in decades of theoretical advances in international trade theory, were based on the notion that the country should produce those goods that were relatively less costly. In the agricultural sector, this would require the abandonment of basic food-grain cultivation in the irrigation districts and other productive areas in favor of high-valued export crops; in this way, the land would be more productive.

As the debate raged in Mexico, the self-sufficiency argument lost ground for several reasons; perhaps the most telling was that it would have involved the strengthening of peasant communities and the transfer of resources to these areas to ensure their continued viability. Justifying the final decision on grounds of efficiency and a growing need for foreign exchange, the Mexican federal government chose to modernize agriculture. Public programs and private investors moved to improve communications and introduce new technology, machinery, seeds, fertilizers, and other inputs into the productive process. Since the bureaucratic structure was too inefficient and underfinanced to succeed in modernizing the agricultural sector, the doors were opened to encourage the participation of foreign investment in the agricultural input and product markets.

Most official agricultural credit, provided at subsidized rates from national or international sources, was channeled to modern agriculture in the irrigation districts. Nevertheless, it was insufficient to meet the growing demands for commercial agriculture expansion. Many producers were forced to search for other sources of capital, and foreign capital often was available to finance the production of specific products that would be destined to export markets; fruits and vegetables were heavily financed by brokers or directly by large industrial enterprises interested in assuring an adequate supply of raw materials for their operations.[1]

The main determinant of production was the profitability of different crops, itself a reflection of relative price structures. It became dominant once farmers were sensitized to market criteria and the government demonstrated its inability to implement a national production program. The government offered price premiums as guarantees to producers who were willing and able to participate in export production programs or in other commercial agricultural programs aimed at supplying the needs of dynamic domestic industries, such as beer and balanced animal-feed products.

Thus, despite avowed interests in national planning for the agricultural sector and specific efforts to try to assure the domestic production of basic food products, government intervention in the agricultural sector was not really designed to achieve the goal of self-sufficiency. An examination of real allocations of credit, public investment in infrastructure, agricultural research, and subsidies for modern agricultural inputs shows that the bias is decidedly in favor of commercial export-oriented agriculture. When these internal advantages are joined with the growing volume of foreign resources available for agricultural production, it is clear why most modern farmers in Mexico are participating directly in industrial and export-oriented agriculture rather than in the production of basic agricultural products for domestic consumption.

Technology and Product Mix

The theory of comparative advantage made itself felt throughout the rural economy. In 1964, the United States decided to permit substantial imports of Mexican cattle on the hoof; perhaps it was coincidental that the U.S. government declared Mexico free of transmissible cattle diseases in that year at the same time that increasing pressures for beef consumption within the United States (partly related to the Vietnam War) were driving up prices in that country. Since the initial exports, the number of head of cattle exported live for fattening with cheap U.S. grain in American feedlots has risen rapidly, so that, by 1978, it had reached 850,000 head of young cattle and more than $65 million in processed meat. Cattle production for the domestic market has been displaced from northern grazing lands to the southern part of the country, where hundreds of thousands of hectares of prime tropical rain forest have been cleared of natural vegetation for the extensive pasturing of low-quality cattle for the domestic market.[2]

Foreign capital stimulated the planting of melons, strawberries, tomatoes, and many other products in the new irrigation districts opened up by the Ministry of Water Resources, especially in the regions of El Bajio and the Northwest. Industrial investments by foreign capital added further stimulus to this tendency by building other processing plants for high-valued, labor-intensive products; in addition to winning export markets, some of these products were able to penetrate the more affluent segments of the Mexican market.

Accompanying these obvious export opportunities were fundamental changes in Mexican industry. New investments in special balanced feeds for livestock – beef, pork, and poultry – led to new industrial processes for meat production in Mexico; fundamentally affecting pork and poultry, the changes meant the switch from artisanal methods to industrial production. This required the planting of vast areas of sorghum as an animal feed, a product that rapidly replaced corn in the more modern parts of the country, given its higher net monetary yields per hectare. Animal feeds and other industrial products (for example, barley) became increasingly important as substitutes for traditional products in those areas where cash cropping of other higher-valued products had not become general.

Coffee exports became very significant by the mid-1970s because of the dramatic increase of prices in New York, but very little of this windfall profit wound up in the pockets of the peasant producers. The government claimed a large part of it in taxes, and the large foreign marketing firms operating in Mexico were able to accumulate another sizable part of the total. Traditional export crops – cotton and sugar – became somewhat less important in relative terms, and, in the 1980s, the country was obliged to import sugar because of stagnant yields and increasing domestic consumption.

By the mid-1960s, price supports were no longer providing incentives for basic food products. Increasingly, large areas of rain-fed lands in traditional agricultural areas were taken out of production. As a result, national production of basic grains – corn and wheat – stagnated and even declined in some years; in 1980, the country was obliged to import almost half of its total requirement for these products.

The Agricultural Work Process and Decision Making

Modernization accompanying the internationalization of capital has had a profound impact on work relations throughout the agricultural sector. Perhaps the most important change has been the displacement of decision making about the crops to be sown from the individual farmer to institutional forces, with an increasingly international character. This change is partly the result of the need for more working capital in agriculture for machinery, chemical inputs, and packaging. Since the narrow margins in farming – even in modern agriculture – force most farmers to obtain financial assistance so that they can continue to produce, the availability of credit for particular crops is determinative. In Mexico, official credit resources have been channeled disproportionately into commercial production and away from basic production of human foodstuffs, despite repeated official declarations to the contrary. Most credit for primary production still comes from the private sector, however – private banks, industrialists, farmers, exporters, and international buyers. This clearly stimulates the production of fruits and vegetables, industrial grains, and livestock and leads farmers to abandon basic food production or induces them to work as laborers in commercial operations and leave their own farms idle.

Another influence propitiating the change in decision making is the attempt to conduct local planning in irrigation districts. Although nominally an exercise in local democracy, in reality agricultural planning is a bureaucratic financial mechanism to impose productive decisions on farmers. Financial assistance and water rights are denied those who attempt to plant outside the guidelines, which generally reflect hopes to exploit profitable export markets and favorable commercial opportunities within the country, rather than to produce basic agricultural commodities for the majority of Mexicans.

Together with decisions about the products to be produced, the farmer is often told how to produce and from whom to obtain needed inputs and services. Financial sources often dictate the purveyors of basic fertilizers (or supply them directly) and the people who will plow the land or fumigate the crops. Thus, the farmer in commercial agriculture finds himself operating basically as a local manager, without much independent decision-making authority. Once the basic choice of crops has been made, most of the rest of the decisions follow in lock-step fashion. The farmer simply implements the inevitable train of events needed to try to get profitable yields; he operates in an uncertain environment, where the timely delivery of key ingredients is beyond his control and where lack of reliability often proves treacherous.

In this environment, work is controlled and workers find themselves transformed into proletarians – in essence if not in form. In many parts of Mexico, the government and the banks and other financiers attempt to maintain the facade of independent peasant producers. This is necessary in order to maintain or shift the risk of failure to the producer, even while the profits are being siphoned off. It is also essential because of the historical heritage of the revolution, the inalienable legal title that many peasants have to their land,

and the combativeness of peasants as a social force in many parts of the country. Although the peasants work their land, however, they do not make any of the decisions about the work process or the use of their time; nor do they have much to say about the distribution of their product.

The growing trend toward productive specialization in export production not only affects the modernized areas; by making subsistence agriculture an increasingly untenable way of life, it also gradually destroys traditional peasant communities. The relative productivity of these groups suffered dramatically as the prices of the goods they produced were fixed and the prices of the goods they had to purchase rose. Technically, the terms of trade turned even more against the peasant producers, heightening incentives for people to abandon traditional areas and leading to an abandonment of lands that may now amount to as many as eleven million hectares, or almost three-fourths of the total land currently in cultivation. For the millions of peasants left underemployed and the millions of hectares of land left idle, the result of the internationalization of agriculture is not a choice between two productive alternatives but rather a wasteful route to social and political disintegration.

Vulnerability to International Forces

The export opportunities to which the farmers and peasants respond offer the promise of great rewards – excellent prices, calculated in dollars, when compared to the lower levels generally received in Mexico. Moreover, most of the costs are financed, in one form or another, by the potential buyers or their representatives, who also provide technical assistance, seeds, and other improved agricultural inputs. The farmers become enthusiastic supporters of the export economy and avid searchers for more credit to expand their production. This demonstration effect creates its own cycle of expansion, which often threatens the very prosperity that sparked it in the first place; as more land is brought into the production of the export product, the foreign buyers can become more selective in the products they purchase and can reduce the prices they pay, thus reducing profit margins and subjecting farmers to strong competitive pressures among themselves. This internal competition often is compounded by variations in the international market for the export products, variations that can transform a prosperous region into a disaster area literally overnight, as has happened in cotton-producing areas in Mexico and is likely to occur in some of the marginal coffee zones.

The boom-or-bust nature of some export production, of course, is not necessarily a general rule for all export products – and it has also spread to other products aimed entirely at local markets, such as pork – but it does exemplify the susceptibility of the economy and its people to market forces beyond their control. These commodity cycles are not only the result of the interaction of demand and supply, which appear as impersonal exchange on national or international markets; they are also the product of an often desperate competition among primary producers to obtain larger shares of stagnant or slow-growing markets or perhaps even of manipulative attempts by oligopolistic forces. Internal economic fluctuations and political pressures in developed capitalist markets also may have sudden and unpredictable effects on the very physical well-being of farmers who are exposing their fortunes exclusively to commercial production.

As part of the same process, a substantial portion of agricultural resources becomes less productive. Recent estimates suggest that as much as half of all the rain-fed land in the country that has already been opened to cultivation is idle, and an equal or greater proportion of peasants is underemployed as a result of the lack of support for traditional agriculture. This is the consequence of policies that make it economically unattractive for the peasants to work their own lands and to produce traditional basic crops to feed the masses; the lack of job opportunities in the industrial sector further aggravates the situation, since peasants are also unable to find employment that would permit them to purchase their means of subsistence.

Agro-industrialization

The internationalization of capital creates another important source of change in the social relations of agricultural production – the modernization of the food industry in Mexico, which is displacing traditional food processors and is expanding directly into the rural areas to influence productive decisions and thereby guarantee supplies of needed agricultural inputs. This process of agro-industrialization affected fruit and vegetable production first and most thoroughly. At first, export interests were particularly important, but the subsequent growth of processing and packaging plants for the internal market led to more stable relations between some of the bigger producers and the industrial users of agricultural products. Perhaps the area where this process has been most rapid and profound, however, has been in the commercial marketing of processed foods for animals. The expansion of balanced-food production, especially for the commercial raising of poultry and pigs, leads to the displacement of corn by sorghum, creating both unemployment and substantial new needs for pesticides, with consequent environmental problems and human food scarcities for mass consumption.

Industrial production of pork and chicken meat reflects a profound change in Mexican industry and agriculture. Previously produced in an isolated setting, the animals were fattened on the leftovers from domestic endeavors, with some grains cultivated expressly for them. With increasing demands and oligopolistically controlled marketing channels, new production techniques and mechanisms to concentrate and centralize control over production were needed. Furthermore, a new internationalized industry – animal feeds – was created, full-grown, to organize production more efficiently and to assure direct industrial control over primary activities. Although, in some cases, individual small-scale farmers actually do the work – that is, grow and fatten the chickens and pigs – their work is organized, financed, and then collected by others, who realize the marketing and distribute the profits.

Meat production organized in this fashion represents an important change in the agricultural sector. It is no longer possible for the isolated farmer to engage in these activities on his own. They are too costly and require substantial inputs, which are not readily produced or used on a small scale – incubators, high-quality reproducing hens, fertilized eggs, medicines, growth hormones, and the balanced foods themselves. Although it is possible for poultry producers to mix the feed and produce their own eggs, experience has shown that, unless they have appropriate marketing connections, they will be at a competitive disadvantage (that is, receive a lower rate of profit) compared to the large, integrated operations; even with pork production, in which reproductive stock is more readily accessible, marketing remains an important bottleneck for the individual producer who would like to become a commercial producer.

In meat production, as in fruit and vegetable production before it, the modernization of agriculture has meant, therefore, the increasing control of the productive process by industrial capital. Even when the actual work must be or still is carried out by individual independent farmers or groups of farmers, the reality is that most of the decisions about how to produce, where to obtain resources, and even how to use the labor of the direct producers have been taken out of their hands.

This tendency seems likely to continue. As industrial processing becomes an increasingly important part of the food industry, the farmers will not be able to market produce directly. Commercial packaging represents an important change in the food industry, symptomatic of far-reaching changes in production, distribution, and consumption. On the production side, it means that the industrial processor makes decisions about the labor process in both industry and agriculture. Distribution is becoming highly organized, requiring greater investment. This leads to the gradual monopolization of marketing by large, vertically integrated enterprises and to important changes in diet to conform to the need for standardization, the demands of large-scale transport, perishability, and the like; it also inevitably means that a smaller proportion of expenditures on food will actually flow back to the primary producer.

This process is very important in the internationalization of capital. It is essential that these changes become widespread if transnational corporations are going to participate in the domestic markets of modernizing countries. It is no wonder, then, that they play an important role in the internationalization of diets. This requires the introduction of new products and consumption standards that focus on the need to change diets. In the process, traditional cuisines are denigrated as solutions to feeding a population; these local variants are rarely as amenable to mass production, standardization, and monopolization. Only in this way can international capital participate directly in the extraction of surplus value, not only through the price mechanism of international trade (for items that enter into world commercial channels) but also within each country as it reorganizes production and consumption to its own convenience.

A Summary and a Direction for Change

Capitalism is the dominant mode of production in Mexico, and it is not surprising that international capital has succeeded in penetrating into its remotest regions. In this chapter, I have followed its integration into agriculture – particularly its ability to transform regions where traditional agriculture predominated. This advance occasioned a striking change in the productive structure of the sector, reorienting land use toward the production of export crops and away from basic food products, which the majority consumes. It also changed the work process, subjecting those farmers who are able to participate in commercial agriculture to a new discipline. This discipline, imposed by capital, dictates the products to be cultivated, the technology to be used, and even the way in which labor is allocated.

As part of this process, agriculture is becoming increasingly tied to industry. Agro-industries often have a determinative role in the organization of production and social relations in the fields. Industry can guarantee a market, provide credit, and supply technical assistance and improved inputs, and therefore can displace traditional agriculture. Meanwhile, the farmer becomes increasingly dependent on and subject to the dictates of industrial capital, often transnational capital. The peasant finds himself even more isolated and less capable of remaining self-sufficient and independent.

The transnational corporation plays an important role in this process, providing the capital and organizational models for the transformation that is taking place. It aggressively expands into new markets and attempts to shape the institutional arrangements that might otherwise unduly limit its ability to continue expanding. Through competition, the transnationals create new products, which they then spread around the world, forging new standards of uniformity that the inexorable power of the market imposes over local and regional variation.

It would be a mistake, however, to blame the transnational corporation for this phenomenon. As a group, the corporations clearly are speeding the advance of capitalism into the Third World. They are active participants in and beneficiaries of the process of forging a single, global capitalist market. It would be erroneous to believe, however, that the control of the transnationals' activities or the demands to make them socially responsible will change the results.

The corporation is prospering on a global scale by taking advantage of opportunities offered by each of the nation-states participating in the worldwide integrative effort. Mexico, like many of the other states in the system, appears to welcome and even encourage the process. In fact, domestic progress is measured in terms of the spread of the international market internally. The accumulation model is based on reproducing locally the economic structures of the developed countries. The transnational corporation is an important and powerful actor, but, without the acquiescence of national governments committed to integrating their countries into the capitalist market, their activities would be greatly circumscribed.

It is not surprising, in such a setting, that marginal groups, condemned to increasing immiserization, search for alternatives. In Mexico, the scenario is taking form: peasants are reorganizing the decrepit organizations that were the basis for collective work, to defend their right to the land and to demand financial and technical support for technologizing their traditional economies. In the face of internal conflicts and produced inflation as a result of the changing productive structure, the nation is being forced to reexamine its development strategy. Although progressive insertion into the capitalist market is still the order of the day, changes are now required even to maintain the existing system; for example, the country recently attempted to prohibit exports of cattle and meat, occasioning some temporary increases in meat prices in the U.S. market and reducing, at least temporarily, the rate of growth of meat prices in Mexico.[3]

Because of the contradiction created by insufficient national production of basic foodstuffs amidst an abundance of human and natural resources to produce these products, some progressive groups support a peasant-based alternative responsive to ideas of national and regional self-sufficiency. This would require a profound reallocation of resources but not an abandonment of export agriculture, since the country has such an abundance of natural resources. Peasant struggles for self-determination might be part of a larger struggle for an alternative to the internationalization of capital. Peasant communities must find alternatives to their full integration into the capitalist economy – which offers inadequate material rewards and no security. Therefore, their struggles might be considered a progressive contribution to efforts to recreate a historically outmoded form of social organization. Such a reconsideration of the role of the peasantry might also provide a new basis for reflecting on the reorganization of productive and regional structures.

Notes

1. It is interesting that, in the face of inadequate resources, domestic industrial enterprises also found that they had to intervene directly at the farm level to finance production or to provide other types of production incentives. They provided price premiums or organized special marketing institutions to guarantee a supply of the agricultural products they needed; in many instances, they claimed that the added costs of these measures were small in comparison with the costs and risks related to the uncertainty occasioned by dealings with the national marketing and price support agency, CONASUPO. For more information on this and related issues, see Barkin and Suarez (1982).

2. For a lengthy discussion of this process, see Barkin (1978).

3. Minor adjustments in public policy were an insufficient response to peasant demands for more resources and better prices for their products and to the critical shortage of basic food products. Political pressures required a new policy, and the Mexican Food System (SAM) was announced in early 1980 as a response. On the basis of two years' experience, an analysis of this reform effort is now possible. The most striking impact of the SAM is the dramatic increase in production, which is a result of (1) the substantial changes in relative prices to favor grains, (2) the reallocation of income from petroleum exports to agriculture, and (3) the most timely and abundant rains in decades. Much of the increased production appears to have come from commercial farmers in the most productive parts of the country, although peasant farmers also increased production significantly. These gains, however, have come at the expense of substantial declines in Mexico's export earnings from agriculture, creating additional pressures on the counry's balance of payments.

Even without going into a more detailed discussion of the SAM, it is possible to suggest some lessons to be learned from the experience. It is partly the result of effective peasant pressures for change resulting from their (correct) analysis of the lack of alternatives offered by the prevailing development strategy. Like most reformist efforts of this type, however, once these pressures were acknowledged rhetorically, most resources were allocated to reinforcing the prevailing pattern of capital accumulation and distribution of power. Without more profound social and political changes, however, long-run food self-sufficiency will remain an elusive and troublesome goal.

References

Barkin, David. 1978. *Desarrollo Regional y Reorganizacion Campesina*. Mexico City: Centro de Ecodesarrollo and Editorial Nueva Imagen.

Barkin, David, and Suarez, Blanca. 1982. *El fin de la autosificiencia*. Mexico City: Centro de Ecodesarrollo and Editorial Nueva Imagen.

III APPLICATIONS TO DEVELOPED COUNTRIES

8 THE IMPLICATIONS OF INDUSTRY RESTRUCTURING FOR SPATIAL ORGANIZATION IN THE UNITED STATES

Thierry J. Noyelle

This chapter outlines three propositions about the current restructuring of capital and labor in the United States and its impact on spatial organization.

The first proposition is that, over the past fifteen years, the U.S. economy has been experiencing a major structural transformation that is closely related to changes in the international economy. This transformation not only consists of a restructuring of capital, in which domestic employment and output in manufacturing have stagnated relative to parts of the service sector while certain activities of United States corporations have become increasingly internationalized; it also consists of the restructuring of labor – both domestically and internationally – marked by an increased division between highly skilled mental and technical labor and unskilled manual and clerical labor.

The second proposition is that these structural changes in the American economy are proceeding along with a transformation of the economic structure of the U.S. system of cities. The reorganization of manufacturing production and the growth of service activities are altering substantially the economic base of many metropolitan areas and redefining relations of dependence among metropolitan centers.

The third and last proposition is that this urban transformation is thriving on and occurring because of the simultaneous transformation of employment systems within metropolitan labor markets characterized by the emergence of new forms of segmentation.

A major conclusion of this chapter is that a new dual economy is emerging in U.S. metropolitan areas, one that differs sharply from the dual economy of the immediate postwar era during which the dichotomy between monopoly and competitive sector firms constituted the main axis of segmentation. The new dual economy is the result of two new axes of segmentation: (1) the tendency toward increased bifurcation within the large corporation's labor force itself, and (2) the tendency toward increased specialization in the large corporation's use of geographical space.

The Current Transformation of the U.S. Economy

The Underlying Crisis

At the root of the current crisis of U.S. capitalism is its inability to continue on with the model of development it had been following since the 1920s and 1930s. This model, referred to by Aglietta (1979) and others as "Fordism," was characterized by (1) the mass production of consumer goods (housing, appliances, automobiles) by way of a technical division of labor based on the semi-automatic assembly line, which emphasized new forms of control over blue-collar workers (internal labor markets – discussed later) and superseded simpler, Taylorist forms of work; (2) the rise of mass consumerism as a means of unlocking the fetters of a previous underconsumptionist era and as a new social ideology that would supersede the earlier Protestant ethic of thrift and self-effacement; (3) the development of an extensive welfare apparatus that would alleviate some of the most negative consequences of capitalist growth; (4) the development of an industrial-military complex that would provide for an engine of economic growth and would backup U.S. domination over the Western world; and (5) a set of political, military, monetary and economic relationships that would permit U.S. firms to continue exploiting Third World nations' resources in raw materials and, later on, to penetrate foreign consumer markets, mostly in the Western European countries.

The two preconditions to this model of development were the making of a new domestic social order and the consolidation of American political and economic dominance throughout the capitalist world in the aftermath of the Great Depression. Domestically, the strengthening of the class alliance between big business, big government and big labor followed in the postwar era the general directions laid out by Roosevelt and the New Deal liberal reformists. Internationally, World War II established the unquestionable nature of U.S. hegemony over other capitalist nations, permitting U.S. multinationals to expand abroad and the U.S. economy to extract some of the surplus necessary to pay for the costs of maintaining stability at home and abroad.

By the late 1960s, however, the model was beginning to unravel for several reasons (Aglietta 1979; Bloch 1977): (1) the mounting challenge from Third World nations to regain political independence and control over their own resources (namely, the copper crisis of the late 1960s and, more importantly, the oil crisis of the 1970s); (2) the mounting challenge of non-U.S. corporations to U.S. multinationals, reflected in European, Japanese, and some Third World firms undercutting not only foreign markets once dominated by U.S. firms but also, by the early 1970s, the U.S. domestic market; (3) the increasing strain placed on the dollar-dominated international monetary system by the chronic deficit of the U.S. balance of trade and payments, because of the increasing burden of maintaining the military apparatus, the dependence of the U.S. economy on foreign sources of oil, and the loss of competitive position by U.S. firms; (4) domestically, the strain on the model of mass consumerism laid out after the 1920s; (5) the strain placed on the assembly line model of work, which prevailed until the late 1960s, both because of the increasing competition from cheap foreign labor sources and because of the increasing resistance of U.S. workers to this model of work (as manifested by the rise of absenteeism, the rise in strike activity, shoddy workmanship, and decline in productivity); and (6) the emerging financial crisis of the welfare apparatus. In short, these various crises meant the beginning of the demise of the international-domestic economic order under which U.S. capitalism had operated throughout most of the postwar era and signaled a period of fundamental transformation based on the acceleration of the internationalization of U.S. capital, its domestic redeployment, and labor market restructuring.

The International Redeployment of U.S. Capital

Before World War II, large U.S. industrial corporations had used foreign direct investment almost exclusively as a way of obtaining the primary materials (oil, mineral, food) they needed to operate some of their domestic operations from abroad. In the aftermath of the war, the focus of the internationalization of large U.S. firms shifted to the use of foreign direct investments as a way of directly penetrating foreign consumer markets through local production.[1] Large U.S. corporations put their resources to work in other nations or regions of the world to set up full-blown, regionwide, autonomous systems of production facilities with which they could cash in on expanding consumer markets (mostly in Western Europe and to a lesser extent in some of the Latin American countries). During this period, duplication within the firm between domestic production facilities and those established abroad became the rule. The trend setters were companies such as General Motors or IBM, which assembled cars or computers in Europe using parts and supplies that, for the most part, were produced or purchased locally. Intrafirm international trade of manufactured goods remained limited, indicating little relationship among production facilities located in separate markets.

In the 1970s, a new and different process of internationalization emerged,[2] largely as a response to two of the main threats placed on the dominance of U.S. firms: the growing competition of goods produced with cheap labor by a few fast-growing Third World nations (Taiwan, Hong Kong, South Korea, and so on) and the increasing penetration of European and Japanese multinationals into once-reserved American markets. As market barriers began falling under the pressure of renewed competition, the issue for many U.S. firms rapidly became one of either competing with foreign firms on the same labor cost basis or moving out of unprofitable activities.

As a result, a new international division of labor began unfolding, both within and among major corporations. This new division of labor has a world dimension in at least two respects. First, because of U.S. firms' disinvestment from certain areas of industry, the U.S. economy is becoming increasingly specialized in terms of the goods and services it produces, with a tendency to specialize in some of the most technologically sophisticated areas.

Second, in industries in which U.S. capital has chosen to continue to compete, firms are proceeding to restructure their production processes by reducing the direct costs of production and generating economies of scale by operating on a world scale. (See chapter 9 for the example of the automobile industry.) This is done by eliminating the redundancies that exist among the firm's domestic and foreign-based facilities and by reorganizing the division of tasks within and among them, so that widely dispersed factories may now be brought to operate as part of a worldwide system of production facilities in which parts are produced in one country, then shipped to and assembled in another for the purpose of selling final products in consumer markets that are now conceived on a worldwide basis. Thus, intrafirm trade becomes a growing component of international trade as companies ship their products from one facility to another.

This process places heavy emphasis on bringing Third World nations into the production space of large U.S. corporations in order to benefit from the low wages characteristic of such areas (Trajtenberg, undated), although it does not rule out certain forms of production within the most developed economies, where labor costs are much higher. The facilities that are more likely to be relocated in cheap labor areas — whether they be Third World nations or underdeveloped regions of advanced countries — are those in which the technical division of labor can be reorganized most easily to require largely unskilled labor (usually assembly work, in which large-scale automation can be introduced). By comparison, production establishments in which processes of manufacturing continue to be highly technical and to require skilled labor remain in the most developed regions, where engineering or technical services and pools of skilled labor are close at hand (Noyelle and Stanback 1981). This distinction is fundamental in understanding the ongoing restructuring of the U.S. urban system.

Domestic Redeployment of U.S. Capital

This process of worldwide reorganization is translating into four major changes in the domestic operations of U.S. corporations, which go a long way in explaining the observable shift to services in the U.S. economy. These changes involve (1) a process of domestic disinvestment out of some of the older manufacturing industries, such as garment or steel, a process that not only is leaving these markets increasingly open to foreign corporations but is having a dramatic impact on workers' displacement in older manufacturing centers, such as Youngstown, Johnstown, and so forth (Shapiro and Volk 1979); (2) a process of domestic employment contraction and reorganization in other traditional manufacturing sectors, such as the automobile industry, in which U.S. firms have decided to continue operating, resulting in a substantial transformation in the kinds and numbers of manufacturing jobs that will be left at home once the reorganization is achieved (Cohen 1981); (3) the reinvestment of freed-up capital into more profitable areas of manufacturing (electronics, telecommunications, energy) or services (transportation, fast food, health); and (4) a dramatic increase in the demand for financial and other producer services (accounting, law, consulting, and the like) attending to the new requirements of managing worldwide corporate organizations, resulting in the very rapid growth of employment and output in these activities, both in-house (within the large corporation itself) or out-of-house (among producer service firms) (Stanback et al. 1981).

To evaluate the rise of services in the domestic economy, one needs to understand clearly that services encompass several types of activities that are very different from one another in terms of the role they play in the overall economy, their internal structure, and their labor force requirements. Six major service groupings are distinguishable on the basis of types of outputs (intermediate or final) and institutional settings under which services are provided (private, public, or nonprofit).[3] Distributive and producer services refer to intermediate inputs to the production process. Distributive services are the activities involved in distributing goods and services, mostly at the intermediate output level, either among producers or from producers to retailers. These services include the industrial classifications of transportation, communications, utilities, and wholesale trade. Producer services are activities that assist user firms in carrying out administrative, developmental (research and development, strategic planning), and financial functions: banking, insurance, real estate, accounting, legal services, consulting, advertising, and so forth. (Firms providing distributive and producer services often provide for the needs of the final consumer as well; however, the principal role of the firm determines its classification.) Services considered as final outputs include the industrial classifications of retail services, consumer services (hotels, auto repairs, motion pictures, and so on), nonprofit services (health and education), and government.

Table 8-1 presents changes in the shares of employment and GNP in the various service and nonservice sectors of the economy during the postwar period. In employment terms, what is most dramatic when contrasted with general notions is that retail and consumer services, popularly regarded as the most important activities involved in the growth of services in the U.S. economy, have not grown rapidly, whereas producer services have, as have health, education, and public sector services. In GNP terms, one finding stands out: between 1947 and 1977, the share of GNP of the two groups of services described as intermediate outputs – distributive and producer services – grew from 29 percent to over 36 percent. As Stanback et al. (1981) have argued, these trends reflect the dual transformation undergone by the U.S. economy during the most recent decades – a transformation in *what* the economy produces and in *how* it produces.

In terms of what the economy produces (final outputs), the shift to services has implied a major increase not so much in free-standing services as in services provided along with goods, whether it be advertising, styling, payment plans, warranty plans, or expert advice of the retailer. This complementarity between services and final goods underlies the trend toward product differentiation that has come to characterize consumer markets in the 1970s and 1980s and that reflects the increasing income segmentation of consumer markets, the increasing emphasis of producers on opening new markets and preserving market shares under conditions of increased market saturation, and the attempts to transform the earlier, bland consumerism of the postwar era into a more appealing model of consumption.

In terms of how the economy produces, the increasing importance of producer services and other intermediate service inputs reflects corporations' need to devote greater resources to research and development, to the planning of the different phases of the product cycle, to the coordination of different product lines, or to the management of the corporate institution's growing complexity.

In short, these trends indicate that, although the United States has remained very much a goods-oriented society, it is an economy in which service activities have come to play a very important role, partly because of their complementarity to final goods, partly because of the need to deal with the

Table 8-1. Percentage Distribution of Full Time Equivalent Employment and Gross National Product by Industries: 1947, 1969, and 1977 (in 1972 dollars)

	1947		*1969*		*1977*	
	Employment	*GNP*	*Employment*	*GNP*	*Employment*	*GNP*
Agricultural, extractive, and transformative	*43.39*	*37.38*	*35.09*	*35.99*	*31.60*	*32.81*
Agriculture	4.31	5.57	1.74	3.06	1.90	2.87
Extractive and transformative[a]	39.08	31.81	33.35	32.93	29.70	29.94
Manufacturing	32.27	24.53	27.66	25.60	24.10	24.18
Services	*56.61*	*62.68*	*64.91*	*64.03*	*68.40*	*66.09*
Distributive services	13.54	13.36	10.97	15.00	11.36	16.51
Producer services	6.06	15.50	10.03	18.26	11.96	20.12
Retail services	12.57	11.06	13.00	9.78	14.18	9.89
Mainly consumer services	7.67	5.47	5.75	3.35	4.99	3.11
Nonprofit services[b]	2.61	2.67	4.67	3.58	6.34	4.04
Government and government enterprises	14.16	14.62	20.48	14.07	19.57	12.43
	100.00	100.00	100.00	100.00	100.00	100.00

[a]Includes mining, construction, and manufacturing.

[b]Public education (grade school and state colleges) is included in government.

Sources: U.S. Department of Commerce, Bureau of Economic Analysis, *The National Income and Product Accounts of the United States, 1929–74 Statistical Tables* and *Survey of Current Business*, July 1978.

increasing complexity and size of firms and markets, and partly because direct production of goods for domestic consumption is increasingly carried out abroad.

The Restructuring of Domestic Labor Markets

To analyze the transformation of labor markets that accompanies this restructuring of capital in the domestic economy, I start from the concept of segmented labor markets (Doeringer and Piore 1971; Gordon 1972; Edwards, Reich, and Gordon 1975).[4] According to David Gordon (1979), it is possible to summarize the main kinds of jobs in the U.S. economy as follows:

> *Independent primary jobs:* Technical, professional, managerial, and craft jobs; requiring some general skills and problem-solving abilities; high pay with some job security; rewards to personal characteristics of initiative and general analytic ability. Technical and professional jobs fed by labor markets beginning with the formal education screening process and then reproduced through screening process based both on credentials and work experience. Craft jobs still fed through apprenticeship systems.
> *Subordinate primary jobs:* Decent pay and substantial job security; low general skill requirements; some skills learned on the job through experience; authority relations and internal job structures very important fulcrum for corporate administration of production process and individual's personal advancement. Workers get such jobs through personal contacts as much as through formal labor market processes, and advancement comes much more easily through internal promotion than job-hopping in the external labor market.
> *Secondary jobs:* In small firms or small shops/offices of large firms; low pay; few skills required; no opportunity for advancement; virtually no inducements for workers to remain on the job. Jobs filled through casual and virtually random general labor market shape-ups and advertisement. (Employment offices also feed workers into these jobs.) (pp. 36–37)

What is important to realize is that the second segment, subordinate primary workers, is essentially a product of the social settlement between capital and labor hammered out by the state in the aftermath of the Great Depression. It is also the segment whose very existence is being fundamentally questioned by the transformation at work. In labor market terms, the settlement obtained by large segments of mostly blue-collar workers entailed the general improvement of working conditions to a level thus far never achieved or guaranteed. It offered the recognition of industrial unions as the official bargaining representative of workers, improvement in long-term job stability, recognition of seniority rights, guaranteed increases in real wages, some opportunities for occupational upward mobility and a whole range of additional benefits (pension, health insurance, and so forth). As was first suggested by Doeringer and Piore and is indicated in Gordon's brief description, ladders of upward mobility internal to the firm became one of the cornerstones of this new system of work.[5]

Eventually, this social settlement covered workers in the construction industry, in manufacturing sectors dominated by large or very large firms (such as steel, automobile, or petrochemical), in a few service industries (mostly distributive services), and, to a large extent, in government itself. For a variety of historical reasons having to do with differences in workers' militancy, workers in the old, established, industrial states of the New England, mid-Atlantic, and North Central regions came to benefit the most from this New Deal settlement. On the contrary, workers employed in manufacturing industries dominated by small firms, in most of the service industries, and in the South (for example, in textiles) were largely untouched by this new social contract.

There are at least three important ways in which this postwar labor market structure is being transformed as the U.S. economy moves onto its new phase of development. First, the rise of employment in the service industries is bringing about the development of employment systems with a much thinner intermediate labor segment (primary subordinate workers). As Stanback and Noyelle (1982) have shown, there are differences, however, in the job structure being developed in the six major service industry groups. On the one hand, retailing and consumer services tend to be characterized by an overwhelming concentration of mostly secondary jobs (cashiers, service workers), few primary independent jobs (managers, professionals), and low pay across the entire range of occupations they offer as compared to similar occupations in other industries (including primary independent jobs). In addition, these trends have been accentuated by the penetration of large capital in areas once confined to small businesses, resulting in a greater standardization of products and production processes and a marked lowering of skill requirements (for example, fast food businesses and hotels) (Bailey and Friedman 1981). Distributive and government services, on the other hand, tend to offer a much larger share of primary jobs (both dependent and subordinate) and to pay relatively well across the range of occupations they offer. Finally, producer and nonprofit services tend to fall in between, offering more balanced mixes of primary independent and secondary jobs (mostly office and nonoffice clerical), with somewhat greater employment stability and relatively stronger pay for secondary workers than in the most unfavorable service industries — retailing and consumer services. Here again, however, the drive toward extracting greater productivity from office workers by way of computerized work stations and similar technologies is increasing the dichotomy at work.

The impact of the sheer growth of employment in the services and of the kinds of employment systems that are being created in service industries on the overall labor market structure is quite unambiguous: the tendency is toward an increasing dichotomy between a very large segment of secondary workers and the somewhat narrower one of primary independent workers. This is indicated by Stanback and Noyelle's calculation of the impact of the 1960–1975 employment increases in services on the structure of the distribution of earnings in the U.S.[6] Between 1960 and 1975, the relative number of workers with earnings 120 percent or above the all-worker average increased slightly, from 32 to 34 percent, and that of workers with earnings 80 percent or below the all-worker average grew sharply, from 32 to 38 percent, while the relative number of workers in the medium earning segment decreased dramatically, from about 36 to less than 28 percent, as 54 percent of the jobs created were in the lower earning segment (with earnings below 80 percent of the average earnings of all workers) and 35 percent in the upper earnings segments (with earnings above 120 percent of the average earnings of all workers).

Second, this trend is being reinforced by the fact that, in both the nonservice and the service industries, there is a continuing shift away from blue-collar occupations toward white-collar occupations – a trend that largely reflects the increasing importance of producer-service-like functions within large service or nonservice corporate organizations (that is, the rise of central offices). It is not surprising that these functions are carried out with a labor force that is typically dichotomized between professionals and managers on the one hand and office clericals on the other.

Finally, within production establishments of industrial firms – once the typical stronghold of primary subordinate workers – the trend is again toward a more dichotomized workforce, between engineers and technicians in the draft rooms and assemblers on the shop floor. This is largely the result of the new technical division of labor that is being put in place in many industries as they shift to a worldwide scale. Thus, these trends are clearly evidenced in the electronics industry, but there is also evidence that, in traditional industries that are being restructured (such as parts of the steel industry or the automobile industry), there are attempts to create out of the old internal labor market structure systems of work that resemble the more dichotomized system becoming prevalent in so many other industries.[7]

For the most part, this major transformation of labor markets has been possible because of a heavy investment in the education of a new generation of primarily white males who have so far received the lion's share of the managerial, professional, and technical jobs opened up by the new economy (with the notable exception of such occupations as nursing and teaching) and from drawing on the largely underutilized supply of women and minority workers to fill up the ranks of mostly clerical and low-skill service worker positions.[8] Indeed, a major story behind this transformation is the staggering growth of women's participation rate in the labor force, which in less than two decades (1965–1980) shot up from less than 35 percent to well over 50 percent.

So far, such structuring of the service industries' workforce – characterized by a strong identification between races, sexes, and occupations – has permitted employers to avoid the formation of a relatively more costly segment of subordinate primary workers in most of these industries. Unionization rates have remained very low among white-collar workers (less than 15 percent, as against 45 percent among blue-collar workers). This relative lack of pressure on employers by workers holding lower occupational jobs has been possible partly because part-time work and big turnover of the labor force in secondary jobs have been used to make organizing difficult, partly because women's earnings have continued to be seen as secondary to those of the household's primary breadwinner, and partly because traditional industrial unions have been largely unresponsive to these new developments. Whether this relative docility of the white-collar labor force is to continue, however, may be a different matter.

The Redeployment of Capital in the U.S. System of Cities

In what ways is the restructuring of capital and labor reflected in the transformation of the U.S. system of cities on the one hand and metropolitan labor markets on the other? The threefold redeployment of U.S. capital suggested earlier (reorganization of production processes, shift of resources to the central offices of large corporations, and expansion of capital in service areas) is closely related to the fundamental restructuring of the economic base of many cities and of the urban system as a whole. A new urban hierarchy is emerging, one in which new relationships of economic dominance are being developed, between service-oriented, decision-making centers on the one hand and production-oriented, dependent centers on the other, that reflect major transformations in the geography of capital.

The Locational Characteristics of Manufacturing Production and Key Service Activities

Two major developments must be kept in mind. The first relates to locational tendencies of manufacturing production, the second to those of key service activities. Since the end of the nineteenth century, U.S. firms have sought ways to avoid high labor costs – whether in terms of wage levels, time lost in strikes, or benefit packages (Gordon 1978). Their strategies have included (1) relocation of factories to suburban locations, mostly at the periphery of large northern manufacturing centers, (2) relocation to the southern part of the United States, (3) a general move away from large centers – regardless of region – toward smaller cities and nonmetropolitan areas, and (4) relocation to underdeveloped nations (see earlier discussion). However, there are profound qualitative differences in the strategies employed, depending on the historical period.

In the earlier postwar decades, the scope of competition within the U.S. economy remained largely restricted to U.S. firms. The opening of the South to the mainstream economy meant that southern labor markets could now be used to compete with northern ones in industries requiring low-paid, low-skilled labor. For the most part, then, the relocation of production establishments away from the traditional northern centers to the South remained limited to industries that relied primarily on low-skilled labor (namely, the southern shift of the textile or the shoe industries), with the North retaining its virtual monopoly over capital-intensive industries. By comparison, the relocation of factories in the suburbs of large northern manufacturing centers was often no more than an attempt by capital-intensive firms dependent on skilled blue-collar labor to weaken workers' power to organize, while remaining close to major pools of skilled labor.

Largely as a result of the increasing opening of the U.S. economy to world competition, predominantly in the late 1960s and the 1970s, firms operating in more capital-intensive industries found themselves under strong pressure to begin relocating certain of their facilities to cheap labor areas. The process that began unfolding involved a reorganization of the division of labor within these firms – essentially, that described earlier in discussing the latest phase of the process of internationalization – characterized by the thrusting outward of certain of their facilities to some of the least developed areas of the nation (southern or smaller urban or nonurban areas) or to Third World nations, and the retention of technical production in older centers, where pools of skilled labor and specialized service inputs (engineering, R&D, product testing) were better developed. In short, much of the industrialization of the South during the postwar era must be seen as a result of both the relocation of labor-intensive, low-paying industries earlier on and the redeployment of the low-wage industrial establishments of firms operating in high-paying industries in the more recent decades (Noyelle and Stanback 1981, ch. 5).

The other major feature of the postwar transformation is the fact that producer services, producer-service-like activities of the corporation (national headquarters, regional headquarters and divisional offices, R&D establishments, and so on), key governmental institutions, and educational facilities have tended to develop mostly in a very selective set of key service centers (mostly large metropolises), in which they have come to dominate the economic life of the locale. Here, as in the case of the redeployment of production facilities, the large corporation has been at center stage, since the multiplication and the relatively limited regional dispersion of administrative and central offices has fueled much of the growth of producer service firms and other key service activities in specific locales (Noyelle and Stanback 1981, ch. 6 and 7).

The principal outcome of these postwar changes has been a sorting out of functions among metropolitan centers (particularly vigorous during the 1970s), leading to a fundamental reorganization not only of the employment base of many cities but of the entire structure of the U.S. urban system.

The New Urban Hierarchy

To study the impact of this transformation on the U.S. system of cities, Noyelle and Stanback (1981) have developed a typology of the 140 largest U.S. metropolitan areas, based on the 1976 employment structure of cities (using service groupings similar to those used earlier) and other key indicators of structure (number of large firms headquartered, banking assets, and so forth).

Their analysis shows the emergence of a three-tiered urban hierarchy, consisting of (1) diversified producer service centers or nodal centers, (2) specialized producer service centers, and (3) dependent centers.[9]

First-tier cities are characterized by large concentrations of national and regional headquarters of large corporations, well-developed banking facilities, dense networks of producer service firms (insurance, accounting, advertising, legal counsel, public relations, and so forth), and, most often, important educational, medical, and public sector institutions (for example, New York, Los Angeles, Philadelphia, Dallas, Atlanta, or smaller cities, such as Charlotte or Omaha). They are also important centers for wholesale distribution of manufactured goods. By comparison, the service specialization of second-tier cities tends to be more narrowly defined. Most of these cities are specialized in management and technical production for well-defined industries (for example, Detroit in automobiles, San Jose in semiconductors, Rochester in office equipment, Pittsburgh in steel) and, as such, are characterized by concentrations of national headquarters of large firms in those industries and the head offices of their major industrial divisions, R&D facilities, and technically oriented production establishments. In addition, a group of these second-tier cities is specialized in providing government services. In general, large firms headquartered in second-tier cities must obtain producer services, such as banking or advertising, from firms located in first-tier cities. Finally, third-tier cities are mostly specialized in the production of manufactured goods or in the provision of consumer-oriented services of a resort or residential nature. First- and second-tier cities tend to be large or medium-sized population centers, while third-tier cities are usually smaller areas, although there are important exceptions to this rule.

Noyelle and Stanback's (1981) analysis of recent developmental trends in each of these major types of cities suggests that the basic structure of this new urban system is likely to develop in directions that will further sharpen the current differentiation among major types of cities. Thus, key services are likely to continue to grow almost exclusively in cities of the first two tiers, while the dependent centers are likely to remain highly specialized (and therefore vulnerable to economic swings) either in production activities or in consumer services.

The basic principles underlying the dynamics of this three-tiered structure are thus simple. The first two tiers include those centers in which large corporate or public sector institutions make decisions regarding growth and development in the nation and its many urban economies, whereas the third tier includes cities that are largely subordinate to the decisions taken in the former two tiers. The second and subsidiary principle is that direct production and especially assembly work are now increasingly relegated to cities of the third tier, although the more technically oriented production establishments tend to remain in centers with better developed technical resources – especially in some of the specialized service centers of the second tier.

The implications of the foregoing discussion are clear. Although the urban system from the turn of the century until the immediate postwar era was characterized by the dominance of large manufacturing centers (mostly, but not exclusively, from the Northeast and North Central regions), the dominance of centers specialized in the production of producer and other key services over the remainder of the urban system defines the structure of the emerging new urban hierarchy. In this new urban system, dominance is defined increasingly by the capacity of these service centers to organize and expand production on a systemwide basis – more and more international in dimension – and increasingly less by their ability to get the goods out locally, as was the case in the past. What is remarkable about this transformation is that many among these new service-oriented centers are the large manufacturing centers of the earlier era, though fundamentally transformed in terms of structure, while only a more limited number of Sunbelt cities seem to be reaching a dominant status.

The Restructuring of Metropolitan Labor Markets

The preceding analysis of the redeployment of capital in the U.S. system of cities suggests that employment opportunities and the resulting structure of local labor markets are likely to vary considerably from place to place. Stanback and Noyelle's (1982) investigation of the labor markets of seven metropolitan areas has led them to argue that, where the transformation of metropolitan economies produces a high concentration of employment in corporate offices, producer services, nonprofit services, and public sector services, there is likely to develop a bifurcated labor market composed of primary independent jobs and secondary jobs; and where metropolitan economies are characterized by the development of employment primarily in consumer services, retailing, or assembly-type production, secondary jobs are likely to predominate. In both cases, subordinate primary jobs – the major channel of upward mobility for labor and the fruits of the earlier, big labor–big business alliance – are likely to be disappearing.

The Stanback and Noyelle study tests primarily the first case, since six of the seven cities they studied can be classified as nodal centers (Atlanta, Denver, Phoenix, Columbus [Ohio], Nashville, and Charlotte). In Atlanta, Denver, Phoenix, Nashville, and Charlotte, there is evidence that local labor markets are highly dualistic, partly because primary subordinate work structures never took a stronghold on these economies, but also partly because the kinds of industries that have developed in these economies in the most recent decades have all been characterized by a strong dichotomy between primary independent and secondary jobs. It is more interesting, however, that, in Columbus – a metropolitan area once typical of the large, unionized manufacturing cities of the Snowbelt region but transforming rapidly into a nodal center – there is clear evidence of a rapid contraction of the intermediate segment of primary subordinate workers and of the development of a local labor market increasingly resembling that of its five southern sisters. In this respect, Stanback and Noyelle's (1982) findings are highly consistent with those of Harrison and Hill (1977), which are based on a comparison of labor market developments in Denver and Baltimore.

The evidence displayed by Stanback and Noyelle with respect to the second kind of metropolitan center is based only on Buffalo as an example of a dependent production-oriented center. As a once major center of production for the automobile and petrochemical industries, located in a strongly unionized region of the country and showing little sign of transformation to a different economic base, the picture of Buffalo's labor market in the mid-1970s continued to reflect the once-sizable influence of primary subordinate jobs in its economy. Their conclusion is that differences are likely to remain in labor market structures between older, dependent production centers (likely to be located in the Snowbelt and specialized in such industries as steel, automobile, and petrochemical) and newer ones (likely to be located in the South and specialized in new industries) for some time at least, but that, as the process of restructuring proceeds in many of these older industries, the economic survival of the older production centers will be increasingly determined by capital's ability to reorganize work and labor markets in such locales. Undoubtedly, such reorganization will involve a frontal attack on primary subordinate jobs and the growth of secondary jobs.

Concluding Remarks

The analysis presented in this chapter suggests that two powerful forces of segmentation have come about with the redeployment of capital in the U.S. economy: a tendency toward an increasing bifurcation of the labor force and a tendency toward a growing polarization of geographical space.

The theme of a dual economy has been used in the past by a number of economists to describe the structural dichotomy that arose after the 1930s between the oligopolistic (or monopolistic) and competitive sectors of the economy (Averitt 1968; O'Connor 1973). In this model, dualism is seen as a result of small competitive firms being driven to operate at the periphery of the very large corporations. Small firms become dependent suppliers of the larger firms and must rely largely on secondary workers if they are to compete. The large firms, in contrast, are characterized by a large segment of primary subordinate workers and a relative ability to isolate themselves from cyclical fluctuations in the economy. Although some of these dimensions of dualism remain, I suggest that new axes of segmentation are coming to the fore as a result of reevaluation by the large corporation of the way it uses geographical space and the way it uses the labor force.

First, the increasing shift in the labor force to white-collar workers, the changes in the labor force of both newer and older manufacturing industries, and the penetration of large firms into producer- or consumer-oriented service areas are all symptomatic of a sharp transformation in the way large corporations are using labor, marked by their much greater reliance on secondary workers. Increased dualism is thus emerging in the form of a much sharper dichotomy between primary independent workers (mostly managers, professionals, technicians) and secondary workers (assemblers in manufacturing, clerical employees, or low-skilled service workers). For secondary workers, this development is accompanied by an increased instability in their position in the labor force. Theirs are essentially dead-end jobs, with very little opportunity for occupational and earnings improvement. Long-term stability of employment in such occupations is contingent upon the ability of employers to keep workers' earnings at low levels and on the ups and downs of the economic cycle. The lack of skill necessary to hold such positions makes layoffs easy during periods of downturns, while competition among workers and the introduction of labor-saving technology represent a constant threat against demands for higher wages.

Second, this structural dualism in the labor force between primary independent and secondary workers is also a geographical dualism – both intra- and intermetropolitan. The analysis presented in this chapter indicates that primary independent workers and the relative economic well-being that goes along with these social strata are found in a relatively restricted number of metropolitan centers (mostly the nodal and specialized service centers). In addition, other research suggests that, within cities where the process of service transformation is the most advanced, there is an increasing spatial dichotomy between those neighborhoods where professional managerial segments enjoy living and those where clerical workers, service workers, and displaced blue-collar workers reside.

Third, the geographical dualism observed in this chapter in terms of the dichotomy between decision-making, service-oriented centers and dependent, production-oriented centers is also a sharp departure from the past. In this respect, it is clear that, although a metropolitan economy's specialization in direct manufacturing production was once a strong positive factor in determining the status of that economy in the larger urban system, it is no longer sufficient to bring about urban dominance. In fact, such development may become a hindrance, relegating centers to a more peripheral position. More broadly, the increasing spatial dichotomy between production and decision-making functions can be understood only in terms of the specificity of the responses of U.S. capital to rising labor costs, declining productivity, and decreasing competitiveness in a period of its development during which the North became increasingly opened to competition, first from other U.S. regions and later from other nations. Accordingly, although many of these developments were inscribed in the particular social and economic dynamics of the postwar period, it is clear that U.S. firms would not have been able to respond to increasing foreign competition without the institutional and technical know-how they gathered from learning how to manage increasingly larger entities during that same period. At the same time, it is clear that U.S. capital's ability to fully develop its response to world competition has been and remains contingent upon its capacity to reconstruct new labor markets that differ sharply from the past and also vary between different types of metropolitan centers.

Finally, this new spatial dichotomy also is important in reinterpreting the growth of the Sunbelt urban system. The westward expansion of urbanization in the United States at the end of the last century and the beginning of this century was based largely on the rise of local entrepreneurship and local capital and the resulting emergence of new dominant manufacturing centers. This factor appears of much less importance in explaining the development of the Sunbelt cities, particularly in the most recent decades, in at least two respects. First, it is clear that large, well-established, northern-based corporations have played a major role in opening up production sites and consumer markets in the Sunbelt. Second, and largely because of the continued dominance of northern institutions in the development process of the Sunbelt, only a few of the new southern urban centers have been able to develop into decision-making centers, while many older, large manufacturing centers have been remarkably successful in repositioning themselves in a renewed dominant status.

From the point of view of the continued expansion of capital, the threat to the stability of this new urban order comes in at least two forms. First, the widening dualism in the labor force is highly conflictual. Not only does this development increasingly negate the ideology of upward mobility that had accompanied the postwar transformation of labor markets, since long-term improvements are no longer guaranteed to large segments of the labor force, but it contributes to the formation of two distinct labor markets and, by extension, two societies separated by enormous social and economic disparities. Second, the economic livelihood of U.S. urban centers is becoming more problematic. The well-being of decision-making centers, in a sense, is based increasingly on the overall stability of the new domestic-international economic order, since a large part of their function is to ensure the circulation and realization of capital that is being produced elsewhere. However, this development comes at a time when the United States is facing increasing difficulties in reorganizing a stable international-domestic economic order. The economic stability of dependent urban centers is becoming more fragile as they find themselves increasingly in competition, not only with one another but with production platforms in Third World nations. These are, of course, only sketches of the highly contradictory nature of current urban developments in the United States that await further analysis.

In conclusion, it should be clear that there is more to industry restructuring than the narrow issues of the de facto bankruptcy of Chrysler or the advent of high-technology firms, publicized by the business press and the daily media. From the point of view of capital, industry restructuring involves not only disinvestment from or reinvestment in specific manufacturing industries but redeployment of capital across the entire range of industrial sectors (including service industries), necessitating choices not only in the domestic economy but also in other countries.

From the point of view of labor, it is clearly extremely urgent to recognize that industry restructuring is proceeding on the basis of a fundamental transformation of work, which involves not only the development of managerial, professional, and technical jobs (the part of the transformation that has been most emphasized) but the growth of an even larger proportion of dead-end jobs. In this respect, we need to understand better how the process of labor market transformation that is occurring in individual cities may conflict with, retard, or promote the process of economic-base transformation. We also need better concepts and theories to analyze the emerging labor market structure. Existing dual labor market theories remain based fundamentally on a blue-collar vision of work, which is largely unable to account for the growing importance of white-collar work (which means not only that more people are being employed in circulating and realizing capital but also that the creation of value and surplus value is achieved in different ways). In addition, these theories have little to say about the changing world of secondary workers. The challenges to understand these changes are enormous and have ominous practical implications for years to come.

Notes

1. For an analysis of the postwar phase of internationalization, see Hymer (1976).

2. For an analysis of the most recent phase of internationalization, see Trajtenberg (undated); Frobel, Heinrichs, and Kreye (1979); and G.R.E.S.I. (1976).

3. From Stanback et al. (1981, ch. 1). This classification is very similar to that of Singlemann (1978).

4. For a recent overview of the field and a good bibliography, see Edwards (1979).

5. See Doeringer and Piore (1971). These ladders can simply be defined in terms of the guarantee of steady improvements in the occupational status of workers or, at least, in their earnings level over the years of the tenure in the firm.

6. From table 3.5 in Stanback and Noyelle (1982), using data from U.S. Department of Commerce, *Survey of Income and Education* (for 1975) and U.S. Bureau of Labor Statistics, *Tomorrow's Manpower Needs, National Industry-Occupational Matrix* (for 1960).

7. See Bernstein et al. (1977, ch. 4). For indications of a similar restructuring in the electrical equipment and automobile industries, see *Productivité et Qualité de Vie en Travail* (1981).

8. This is not to deny the existence of other social forces at work, which have brought increasing numbers of women into the labor force: women's movement demands for women's access to work, a breakdown of the traditional family structure, or the rise of divorce and the single-parent family.

9. See Noyelle and Stanback (1981, ch. 4). This typology yields the following breakdown of the 140 largest cities by type:

Diversified Producer Service Centers or Nodal Centers

National Nodal Centers: New York, Los Angeles, Chicago and San Francisco.

Regional Nodal Centers: Philadelphia, Boston, Dallas, Houston, St. Louis, Baltimore, Minneapolis, Cleveland, Atlanta, Miami, Denver, Seattle, Cincinnati, Kansas City, Phoenix, Indianapolis, New Orleans, Portland, Columbus.

Subregional Nodal Centers: Memphis, Salt Lake City, Birmingham, Nashville, Oklahoma City, Jacksonville, Syracuse, Richmond, Charlotte, Omaha, Mobile, Little Rock, Shreveport, Des Moines, Spokane, Jackson Ms.

Specialized Producer Service Centers

Functional Nodal Centers: Detroit, Pittsburgh, Newark, Milwaukee, San Jose, Hartford, Rochester, Louisville, Dayton, Bridgeport, Toledo, Greensboro, Akron, Allentown, Tulsa, New Brunswick, Jersey City, Wilmington, Paterson, Knoxville, Wichita, Fort Wayne, Peoria, Kalamazoo.

Government-Education Centers: Washington, Sacramento, Albany, New Haven, Springfield, Raleigh-Durham, Fresno, Austin, Lansing, Oxnard-Ventura, Harrisburg, Baton Rouge, Tacoma, Columbus S.C., Utica, Trenton, Madison, Stockton, South Bend, Ann Arbor.

Dependent Centers

Resort-Retirement-Residential Centers: Nassau-Suffolk, Anaheim, Tampa, Riverside, Ft. Lauderdale, Honolulu, Orlando, Long Branch-Asbury Park, West Palm Beach, Albuquerque, Las Vegas, Santa Barbara.

Manufacturing Centers: Buffalo, Providence, Worcester, Gary, N.E. Pennsylvania, Grand Rapids, Youngstown, Greenville, Flint, New Bedford, Canton, Johnson City, Chattanooga, Davenport, Beaumont, York, Lancaster, Binghamton, Reading, Huntington, Evansville, Appleton, Erie, Rockford, Lorain.

Industrial-Military Centers: San Diego, Norfolk, San Antonio, El Paso, Charleston S.C., Newport News, Lexington, Huntsville, Augusta, Vallejo, Colorado Springs, Pensacola, Salinas.

Mining-Industrial Centers: Tucson, Bakersfield, Corpus Christi, Lakeland, Johnstown Pa., Duluth, Charleston W. Va.

Although this typology includes only the 140 largest population centers, there are solid indications from other studies that many among the smaller metropolitan places fall within the dependent centers category. See Goldstein, Paulson, and Bergman (1981).

References

Aglietta, Michel. 1979. *A Theory of Capitalist Regulation: The U.S. Experience.* London: New Left Books.

Averitt, R.T. 1968. *The Dual Economy: The Dynamics of American Industry Structure.* New York: Norton.

Bailey, Thomas, and Friedman, Marcia K. 1981. *Immigrants and Native-Born Workers in the Restaurant Industry in New York City.* New York: Conservation of Human Resources.

Bernstein, Alan; DeGrasse, Robert; Grassman, Rachael; Paine, Chris; and Siegel, Lenny. 1977. *Silicon Valley: Paradise or Paradox?* Mountain View, Calif.: Pacific Studies Center.

Bloch, Fred. 1977. *The Origins of International Economic Disorder.* Berkeley: University of California Press.

Cohen, Robert B. 1981. *The Employment Consequences of Structural Change in the Auto Industry.* Cambridge, Mass.: MIT Project on the Automobile Industry.

Doeringer, Peter, and Piore, Michael J. 1971. *Internal Labor Markets and Manpower Analysis.* Lexington, Mass.: Lexington Books, D.C. Heath.

Edwards, Richard C. 1979. *Contested Terrain: The Transformation of the Work Place in the Twentieth Century.* New York: Basic Books.

Edwards, Richard C.; Reich, Michael; and Gordon, David, Eds. 1975. *Labor Market Segmentation.* Lexington, Mass.: Lexington Books, D.C. Heath.

Frobel, Folker; Heinrichs, Jurgen; and Kreye, Otto. 1979. *The New International Division of Labour.* Cambridge, England: Cambridge University Press.

Goldstein, Harvey A.; Paulson, Nancy A.; and Bergman, Edward M. 1981. *Models of Industry Employment Change for Labor Market Areas.* Study commissioned by the Employment and Training Administration, U.S. Department of Labor, May.

Gordon, David M. 1972. *Theories of Poverty and Underemployment.* Lexington, Mass.: Lexington Books, D.C. Heath.

______. 1978. "Capitalist Development and the History of American Cities." In *Marxism and the Metropolis,* edited by William K. Tabb and Larry Sawers. New York: Oxford University Press.

______. 1979. *The Working Poor: Towards a State Agenda.* Washington, D.C.: The Council of State Planning Agencies.

G.R.E.S.I. 1976. *La Division Internationale du Travail.* Paris: La Documentation Française.

Harrison, Bennett, and Hill, Edward. 1977. "The Changing Structure of Jobs in Older and Younger Cities." Working paper, Department of Urban Studies and Planning, Massachusetts Institute of Technology, December.

Hymer, Stephen. 1976. *The International Operations of National Firms: A Study of Direct Foreign Investment.* Cambridge, Mass.: MIT Press.

Noyelle, Thierry J., and Stanback, Thomas M., Jr. 1981. *The Economic Transformation of American Cities.* New York: Conservation of Human Resources.

O'Connor, James. 1973. *The Fiscal Crisis of the State.* New York: St. Martin's Press.

Productivité et Qualité de Vie au Travail, Compte Rendu de Mission aux Etats Unis. Dossier du Centre d'Etudes et de Recherches sur les Qualifications #27. Paris: La Documentation Française.

Shapiro, Helen, and Volk, Steven. 1979. "Steelyard Blues." *NACLA Report on the Americas* 12, no. 1 (January-February).

Singlemann, Joachim. 1978. *From Agriculture to Services.* Beverly Hills: Sage Publications.

Stanback, Thomas M., Jr.; Bearse, Peter J.; Noyelle, Thierry J.; and Karasek, Robert A. 1981. *Services: The New Economy.* Totowa, N.J.: Allanheld, Osmun.

Stanback, Thomas M., Jr., and Noyelle, Thierry J. 1982. *Cities in Transition.* Totowa, N.J.: Allanheld, Osmun.

Trajtenberg, Raul. Undated working paper. "Transnational and Cheap Labor in the Periphery." Mexico: Latin American Institute of Transnational Studies.

9 THE NEW SPATIAL ORGANIZATION OF THE EUROPEAN AND AMERICAN AUTOMOTIVE INDUSTRIES

Robert B. Cohen

The internationalization of production has destroyed previous national and regional schemes of organizing labor and capital. It has given birth to a new spatial organization of accumulation, closely linked to the new international division of labor. This chapter examines some examples of how the spatial organization of the automotive industry has changed as a result of the process of global integration of production over the last decade. The first part focuses on the recent history of Ford in Europe, as a specific example of how an automobile firm has planned to use its worldwide network of operations to restore its competitive position. The second part of the chapter examines the parallels between Ford's response to changing conditions in Europe and the restructuring of the U.S. automotive industry.

Ford's Strategy in Europe

Ford's strategy in Europe is one of the most interesting cases of adaptation to an integrated global market for production, since it permits us to view the implementation of a strategy that attempts to reposition a major automobile producer in markets where it must compete with the Japanese and large European producers. This plan, called Ford's AJ strategy, attempts to reorient Ford to compete in world automobile markets "after Japan," that is, after the emergence of Japanese automobile producers as major competitors in international car markets.

Ford's ten-year business plan defines the steps that will be taken to bring the company up to the level of its Japanese competitors. These steps focus on ways to improve existing production and to cut costs, largely by reducing the costs of labor and materials. The more-detailed, long-term objective Ford has set for itself concentrates on rationalizing the production network that developed in Europe during the 1970s, when regionalization, rather than international integration, was seen as the key to achieving a dominant position in Europe (Ford of Europe 1980). Ford's long-term objectives underscore the fact that major automakers are not merely adapting to a downturn in the business cycle. Long-term survival will depend on achieving minimum acceptable market shares in key parts of the world and economizing on labor, parts, and new equipment.

Ford has adapted its European operations to implement its long-term objectives in two very different types of markets: the traditional open markets of Scandinavia and the more restricted markets of France, Spain, and Italy. Although Ford succeeded in achieving its desired 14 percent share in Norway in the late 1970s, its market share in most Scandinavian nations has dropped precipitously since the end of 1979, while the Japanese share has grown rapidly (from 16.5 percent, 21.9 percent, and 28.3 percent in Denmark, Norway, and Finland, respectively, to 35.2 percent, 38.7 percent, and 43.3 percent between 1976 and September 1980) (Ford of Europe 1980). Ford's loss of market share in the Scandinavian markets reflects its price disadvantage. Since the Scandinavian markets are not restricted by high import duties, one solution is to market cars produced in less-developed nations, where labor and materials costs are much lower than in Western Europe. Indeed, one of Ford's responses has been to market Brazilian Escorts in Scandinavia ("Ford Special" 1981). Thus, global sourcing of cars becomes a viable alternative in markets where imports are not restricted and price competitiveness can be achieved by low-cost automobile production.

In such countries as Spain, France, and Italy, where imports are restricted by high duties, selling cars imported from an external, low-cost source such as Brazil would have been impractical. In Spain, for instance, import duties on the full built-up cars were 64.6 percent of the imported value in 1972. Thus, another strategy was necessary. In 1972, Ford decided to invest in a new assembly plant in Spain. An examination of this decision, though based on documents from nearly ten years ago, provides a great deal of insight into some of the highly significant cost and market considerations that have led to a restructuring of much of Ford's European operations. Many similar forces may be at work in the restructuring of the U.S. industry, particularly in the pressures now being placed on automobile workers and on parts producers.

Ford invested in Spain not only because of a growing internal Spanish market for cars but also because of a number of important cost advantages in producing for the entire southern European market (which was 40 percent of the western European car market in 1972). Although the cost of building a plant in Spain was more than that of expanding existing capacity in Germany or England, overall production costs at a Spanish facility were lower. Moreover, the cost differentials between Spain and other potential production sites were expected to widen between 1972 and 1985 (Ford of Europe 1972).

Ford's move to Spain reflected the need to reallocate resources on a European scale. Ford had invested in one system of production for Europe in the 1960s and 1970s, but the move to Spain committed it to a reorganized network of facilities for the 1980s that was tied to being competitive in smaller car markets and to gaining a stronger foothold in southern Europe. This signaled a need to change policies toward workers, suppliers, and governments.

A closer examination of some of Ford's documents from the 1972 studies provides a first-hand appreciation of these changes (Ford of Europe 1972). Historically, Ford had been a producer of medium-sized cars in Europe. To produce a small car profitably, it had to reduce costs of production. Thus, one part of the 1972 study focused on comparing labor costs and production costs at a number of Ford facilities, including the proposed "greenfield," or completely new, plant in Spain. One big advantage to producing smaller cars in Spain was the improvement in profitability on sales to France and Italy that could be achieved. Ford was losing $99 for each car it sold in these markets in 1972. This deficit could be cut to $11 by making certain production improvements at existing facilities by 1976, or could even be changed to a profit of $30 per unit by expanding the Ford plant at Saarlouis in Germany. None of these adjustments compared, however, to the $116 profit per car that Ford could obtain by producing in Spain.

As table 9-1 notes, the cost differences between Saarlouis and Valencia were accounted for in three ways. First, direct labor costs in Valencia were 40 percent of those in Saarlouis, although efficiency was 10 percent less. Second, hourly indirect labor costs at Valencia were 53 percent of those in Saarlouis, with efficiency 10 percent less. Third, a subsidy of 13 percent of the export value shipped was to be given by the Spanish government to encourage the growth of exports. Even taking into account the higher shipping and duty costs, and including additional manufacturing costs, Ford's 1972 estimates were that the same car would cost less to produce in Spain than in Germany.

Labor costs and labor flexibility were very important in Ford's decision making. Ford estimated the 1970 to 1980 yearly increases in unit labor costs (changes in wages per hour divided by units produced per hour) for various plant sites. It found that long-run labor costs would increase at a lower rate in Spain than in any other Ford plant location. Ford was also concerned about locating a plant in an area that provided for a significant amount of flexibility

Table 9-1. Cost Comparisons for Producing the Escort 4-Door 1100 Base (1972)

Unit Costs	*Germany (Saarlouis)*	*Spain (Valencia)*	*France (Bordeaux)*
Direct material	$ 701.90	$ 745.51	$ 704.90
Direct labor	145.72	91.33	122.93
Variable overhead	85.42	68.05	79.92
Import tax	–	62.12	–
Variable FCAs	(11.84)	(11.81)	(12.42)
Warranty and policy	28.20	28.20	28.20
Export subsidy	–	(144.82)	–
Export tax	–	16.71	–
Total manufacturing variable cost	$ 952.40	$ 855.29	$ 923.53
Fixed and nonvariable costs	231.00	199.00	218.00
Freight and duty	63.00	131.00	76.00
Interest differential	–	9.00	4.00
Total	$1246.10	$1194.29	$1221.53

Note: The first three costs include estimates of efficiency differences.
Source: Ford of Europe (1972).

in overtime because it faced capacity constraints in other parts of its operations if European sales increased in the late 1970s, as was expected. Thus, the 1972 studies assessed the maximum annual hours, including overtime, that could be achieved at its different assembly plant locations. Here, again, a Spanish plant would have an important advantage over Ford's other sites.

Ford's investment in Spain illustrates two components of its new European strategy. One is the peripheralization of auto production in Europe, with many facilities in central European nations (Germany, Belgium, and France) being downgraded in importance in favor of new plants in peripheral cheap-labor locations. An additional component of Ford's adjustment strategy has been the new significance of investments that are backed by government subsidies or tax breaks. Ford appears to have given this approach a great deal of credibility in reaching its agreement with Spain. It followed this agreement with similar negotiations for British subsidies that offset many of the investment costs for its new engine plant in Bridgend, South Wales, England (Rodgers and Eglin 1977).

Ford's strategy for cost reductions has also included plant-level changes in the way it uses its labor force. Press shop cycles have been cut by 50 percent through improvements in die setting that maintain overall press utilization. First-time capabilities have been improved in paint shops. In-process repairs in body construction and in trim and final assembly were reduced in 1981, eliminating the need for repair stations. Operating penalties that resulted from potential downdays and one-shift operations in continental Europe were minimized in 1981. Workload reductions were achieved in 1981 by simplifying administrative structures and introducing minicomputers on shop floors.

Finally, Ford has attempted to reduce the cost of parts through outsourcing and shifting from double-sourcing of parts to single-sourcing (that is, purchasing parts and components from one supplier rather than from two or more suppliers). Enormous pressures have been placed on suppliers to provide less expensive parts or be dropped from the Ford system. For instance, Ford has turned to its tie with Toyo Kogyo in Japan as an alternative supplier of parts that cannot be produced cheaply enough in Europe, despite freight costs (Ford of Europe 1980).

All the new steps that Ford has implemented in its European operations will have tremendous consequences for workers in Ford's operations and in its suppliers' facilities. The need to measure up to foreign standards increases the likelihood that, if Ford cannot obtain adequate economies by rationalizing its operations and reducing labor and materials costs, it will move its operations to less costly centers. It has already shown an unwillingness to come to a compromise agreement with employees in the Amsterdam plant, where workers strove to prevent a shutdown by converting the facility to a component production center. Ford argued that none of the alternatives proposed would meet its norm of 25 percent return on investment.

Ford's plans to build a new assembly plant in Portugal not only continued the process of peripheralization, placing additional pressure on employees in the older plants in Dagenham and Cologne, but also continued the policy of seeking substantial subsidies from the government. In this case, Portugal has offered $565 million of the total investment cost of $700 million. In addition, Ford introduced a new element into the negotiations by asking for a guarantee of "social peace" from the government if the company chose Portugal over other possible sites in Spain, Austria, and France. This introduces an additional problem for labor in other nations, where unions have rarely considered no-strike agreements as a way of acceding to the needs of management. Ford's moves in Portugal also have pitted several nations against one another in a sort of bidding war for new investments, with little attention being paid to the costs of social dislocation that will result from shifting plants to new sites ("Ford Special" 1981).

Ford's Strategy in the United States

The U.S. automobile industry has experienced a major decline during the last few years. Although most industry observers link the decline in domestic production to the downturn in the business cycle and the increased penetration of

Japanese imports, a number of important structural changes that have taken place are having important impacts on the spatial organization of the industry in the United States.

Regional Employment Shifts

Parallel to the peripheralization strategy in Europe is the U.S. regional shift of automobile plants from the Northeast to the Sunbelt. Previous studies have documented that employment in the automotive industry has shifted to the Sunbelt states and that older, industrial cities have been particularly vulnerable to plant closures (MacLennan and O'Donnell 1980; U.S. Department of Transportation 1980). This analysis is corroborated by statistics for the two 4-digit SIC industries, SIC 3711 (motor vehicles and car bodies) and SIC 3714 (motor vehicle parts and accessories), that make up the auto industry. These data show that growth in the Southeast, Southwest, Plains, and Far West regions accounted for nearly all jobs gained nationwide in assembly operations. Increases in jobs in the Southeast are most visible in the parts industry (see table 9-2). This shift of facilities suggests that automakers are moving to low-wage, less-unionized (or less-militant) areas.

Urban to Rural Shifts

Concerns over problems with traditional industrial workforces may have prompted another trend in the spatial restructuring of the automotive industry in the United States: the Big Three's move to set up new or greenfield plants in places with little history of industrialization – specifically, small towns and rural areas. Certainly, the steps taken by General Motors and other automakers in St. Louis would reinforce this impression.

As documented by MacLennan and O'Donnell (1980), St. Louis will lose between 11,000 and 13,000 autoworkers by 1982, with a large part of these job losses resulting from the relocation of plants to nearby greenfield centers. By mid-1982, all General Motors facilities in the city of St. Louis will be closed, ending jobs in a 60-year old plant that, at its peak in 1978, employed as many as 10,000 workers. General Motors will relocate its Corvette operations to Bowling Green, Kentucky (too far away for workers to commute to), and to a highly automated plant in Wentzville, Missouri, 35 miles from St. Louis. Chrysler and Ford already rely primarily on rural workforces in the St. Louis area. The two Chrysler plants at Fenton, Missouri, are 18 miles from the city, and the main Ford plant at Hazlewood is also outside the city (MacLennan and O'Donnell 1980).

Table 9-2. Geographical Distribution of Employment in the Motor Vehicle Industry

Region	SIC 3711 First Quarter 1975	SIC 3711 Final Quarter 1979	SIC 3714 First Quarter 1975	SIC 3714 Final Quarter 1979
New England	0.7%	1.0%	1.2%	1.1%
Mideast	6.7	6.8	12.0	11.3
Great Lakes	76.1	71.2	70.5	66.2
Southeast	2.6	3.8	7.2	10.7
Plains	6.8	7.8	4.1	4.2
Southwest	1.8	2.9	1.6	2.0
Rocky Mountains	.1	.04	.3	.5
Far West	5.2	6.5	3.1	4.1
U.S. total	335,343	418,458	344,719	415,509

Source: U.S. Department of Labor, Bureau of Labor Statistics, Employment and Wages for SICs 3711 and 3714 (unpublished data).

The move to nonmetropolitan greenfield plants provides automakers access to workforces that are known for their work ethic. A *New York Times* article noted that a Detroit automobile industry executive explained that Volkswagen's selection of New Stanton, Pennsylvania, had much in common with Chrysler's choice of Belleville, Illinois, for its new plant. Both areas have predominantly white populations made up largely of descendants of Eastern European immigrants (Vinocur 1977). Japanese investors in California, a number of which are automakers, often have selected cities with substantial numbers of Japanese Americans because of their belief that such workers, though a distinct minority in the workforce, will help maintain the quality of work (Lindsay 1977).

Thus, the move to nonmetropolitan greenfield plants seems to be related to the new demands for more efficient and profitable production. Automakers appear to have concluded that relocating a number of facilities for down-sized cars to areas without a history of industrialization that have ethnic populations with a strong work ethic provides them with a better chance to meet competition than they would have by remaining in older, industrial cities.

Sourcing of Parts and Components

After down-sizing U.S. cars, the first step in improving fuel economy, automotive firms fundamentally altered the design of cars by shifting to front-wheel drive. This fundamental shift in design required major new components, many of which were procured from abroad to reduce costs. In some instances, the companies supplying components had greater experience than their U.S. counterparts and were low-cost producers. In a number of cases, automakers put considerable pressure on the foreign parts suppliers to produce higher-quality and lower-cost components than domestic suppliers could provide. At the same time, automakers were asking parts suppliers to assume more of the risks and costs of new component development.

Another strategy employed by Ford and General Motors has been to reduce the costs of components produced in the United States. Ford sought to have workers at its Livonia transmission plant alter their work rules to cut production costs. In the face of a threat to replace their transmissions with ones from Japan, workers complied with Ford's demand. In another case, however, when Ford sought to have wages cut in half at its Sheffield, Alabama, aluminum foundry plant, workers refused to comply with Ford's demand, even though this meant that Ford was likely to sell the plant or close it and procure similar engine parts from abroad.

General Motors followed a different tactic at its Hyatt bearing plant in Clark, New Jersey. There, the firm negotiated with workers who wanted to purchase the plant rather than see it closed. To keep the plant open, the new worker-owners agreed to reduce the workforce and to take a one-third cut in pay. The workers also left the United Auto Workers (UAW), the union that had previously represented the plant in negotiations with General Motors.

Thus, the possibility of procuring parts from abroad has changed the outlook for parts production by both U.S. parts producers and the automakers themselves. There are already numerous cases in which parts produced in the United States have been displaced by less-expensive parts produced elsewhere and in which automakers have changed wage levels or working conditions at domestic plants as part of a bargain to keep production in the United States.

Public Subsidies

There are several examples of public subsidization of new investment in the U.S. auto industry in the last few years. The first example was Volkswagen's success in obtaining sizable state subsidies for its New Stanton, Pennsylvania, plant. This pattern was followed by General Motors when it won significant tax concessions and land for agreeing to construct a new Cadillac assembly plant. Other examples occurred when Honda and Datsun obtained important subsidies to construct plants in Ohio and Tennessee. These cases indicate that automakers operating in the United States have been able to follow a strategy of seeking subsidization for new investment, as they have in Europe.

Conclusion

The emergence of greater competition in the world's automotive industry has led to the international integration of automobile production by the world's largest automakers. The opportunity to obtain parts and components from many new centers of production, such as Brazil, Spain, Portugal, and Korea, has created pressures to reduce production costs at home and to restructure the domestic automobile industry in Europe as well as in the United States. As we have seen, there are many parallels between Ford's restructuring of its operations in Europe and some of the recent changes in the U.S. automotive industry – peripheralization and greenfielding, a new sourcing strategy, and the use of public subsidies.

What is likely to happen to the reorganization of the automotive industry in the United States? Two tendencies appear to be contending with each other: either companies move production overseas or they succeed in restructuring U.S. operations by relocating plants to new areas, by changing the cost of components, or by receiving subsidies from states and localities.

References

Doz, Yves. 1979. *Ford in Spain* (A). Harvard Business School, Case 4-380-091.

Ford of Europe, Body and Assembly Operations. 1980. "1980 Controller's Office Review Meeting" (December 18).

Ford of Europe, Finance Staff Volume Planning and Integration Studies. 1972. "Alternatives For the Expansion of Passenger Car Assembly Capacity in Europe." (July 28).

Ford of Europe. 1981. Product letter on the Brazilian Escort. Internal memorandum (January).

"Ford Special." 1981. *Transnational Information Exchange* 9 (April-August).

Lindsay, Robert. "Japanese Beachhead in California." *New York Times,* 21 August 1977, p. F4.

MacLennan, Carol, and O'Donnell, John. 1980. "The Effects of the Automobile Transition on Employment: A Plant and Community Study." Washington, D.C.: National Highway Traffic Safety Administration.

O'Donnell, John P.; Byron, George; and O'Connell, Mike. 1981. "Identifying Automotive Changes in Facilities and Capital Equipment and Assessing Community and Employment Impacts." U.S. Department of Transportation, Office of the Secretary of Transportation, DOT-TSC-OST-81-3, May.

Rodgers, Peter, and Eglin, Roger. "Welsh first team wins new Ford plant." *London Sunday Times,* 9 November 1977.

U.S. Department of Transportation, Office of the Secretary of Transportation. 1980. *The U.S. Automobile Industry* (The Goldschmidt Report).

Vinocur, John. "The Americanization of VW." *New York Times,* 9 October 1977, p. D5.

Conclusion

[illegible]

References

[illegible]

10 LABOR MIGRATION AND THE ROLE OF THE STATE

The Immigration Policy of the Belgian Government

Frank Moulaert

Previous chapters have discussed the two major corporate strategies for reducing labor costs under the new international division of labor: (1) the peripheralization of some stages of production for the world market to countries or regions with comparatively cheap nonmilitant labor; and (2) lowering skill requirements of the work process, which permits increasing bifurcation of labor markets into high-wage and low-wage sectors (see, especially, chapters 8 and 9). In many Western European countries, the second strategy has faced the obstacle of severe shortages of cheap, unskilled labor, given the long history of industrial unionism and rising educational levels of the population. Corporations have addressed this problem not only by relocating some of their production activities to lower-wage countries in the Mediterranean but also by organizing large-scale but regulated migrations of workers from that area. Although corporations have used such migration flows since World War II to satisfy their labor needs — first in mining, later in construction, industrial sectors, and services — it is only since the middle to late 1960s, under the impetus of the new international division of labor, that the pressure for such migration became widespread across industrial sectors and services.[1]

The labor migration strategy followed by corporations to reduce costs in traditional production areas, as well as in the new growth sectors, is particularly interesting to analyze because of its dependence on intervention by the national government (that is, the State, as defined in chapter 4) to regulate the flow of migrant labor. Political economy is particularly suited to this analysis because of its explicit theory of the State.[2] This chapter traces the role of the

State as an arena of class struggle between capital and labor around the immigration issue, specifically examining the history of Belgian immigration policy since World War II to see how this struggle has unfolded and whose interests the State has tended to serve. Included are the results of a statistical analysis of time series and sectoral data on granted work permits to reinforce the argument.

Since the 1930s, poor working conditions have caused a severe labor shortage in the mining sector. Before World War II, the mining industry employed Belgian seasonal workers during winter. However, this reserve labor pool of seasonals soon became insufficient to meet the mines' needs, so that, at the end of the 1930s, contingents of migrant workers from Poland, Hungary, Yugoslavia, Czechoslovakia, and Italy were attracted to work in the mines. After World War II, the government tried in vain to force Belgian workers to come back to work in the coal mines. Finally, the immigration of foreigners was authorized as a last resort: between June 1946 and December 1949 more than 77,000 Italians were hired and employed in the mines.

In 1962, when demand for immigrant labor had spread to all sectors, Belgian-based employers and their organizations pressured the government to abolish the obligation to have a work permit before coming to work in Belgium in order to increase the flow of immigrants. They also encouraged the authorities to extend the recruitment area beyond Italy and Spain.

The employers' organizations were successful in their efforts. Illegal employment was tolerated on the condition that legalization took place afterwards. That condition was demanded by the unions, which hoped to control the immigration flows *post factum* and to give migrant workers the same rights as domestic workers. They so demanded in order to prevent job requirements from being lowered too badly. However, the whole immigration process became very hard for the unions to control.

The slowing down of economic expansion and the worsening of the employment situation in 1966 pressed the unions to demand the halt of labor immigration. Although the unions were successful in making the granting of immigrant work permits mandatory again (February 1, 1967), they never succeeded in forcing the government to close off domestic labor markets to foreigners completely. In fact, employers continued to have access to foreign labor markets, through either illegal or legal channels. The practice of tourist immigration had become so common that the measures of 1967 only diminished but did not abolish this practice. Moreover, since 1965, the legalization of tourist-workers had become harder and harder, so that the total number of illegal workers grew sharply.[3] This reserve pool of workers without any civil and social rights became very attractive for many employers.

On August 1, 1974, in reaction to the severe employment crisis, the government halted all immigration but proclaimed the legalization of existing illegal migrants. This led to the legalization of some 35,000 illegal workers, as well as to a selective stopping of the inmigration flows. Still, thousands of migrants were employed illegally, so that it makes sense to label the present stage in immigration practice as a mixed system of legal and illegal employment.

The laws and regulations underlying the right to work by foreigners in Belgium are the outcome of the negotiation process between the social partners (the unions, the employers' organizations) and the State. This negotiation process took place at the National Consultation Organization on Migration Matters, first the DCVA (Drieledige Commissie voor de Vreemde Arbeidskracht, or Tri-Partite Commission for Foreign Labor Power), later the ARI (Adviserende Raad voor de Immigratie, or Advisory Council for Immigration). Of course, these laws were not the work of the advisory organs; they were determined by parliamentary and executive decisions (royal decrees) by the Ministries of Employment and Justice. Moreover, responsibility for enforcing the laws and executive decrees belongs to the local official employment offices, the Foreigners' Police at the Department of Justice, and the local police. Their practice normally conforms to the legal mandates; but these laws still leave sufficient freedom for interpretation by the executing personnel or for deviant internal instructions issued by "the administration" (the different bureaucracies). We will stay with the analysis of the negotiation process at the consultation organs, however, because what has gone on there is a good reflection of the different positions generally taken by the different partners in the immigration policy struggle.

The Role of the State

The State is regarded in political economy as an arena of class struggle or struggle between the social partners, in which the state organization implements policies and programs to further the goals of the victors. The opposing class interests at stake in the immigration question are the availability of a sufficient reserve of unskilled labor force versus the equal and improved rights for both domestic and foreign workers.

In this approach, the State is not regarded as an actor in social struggle itself. This, of course, is a simplification. In reality, the State acts autonomously to a certain extent. For example, the Foreigners' Police (part of the State Security) often behaves as a state within the state and acts as if it were in its interest that migrants be overcontrolled. This overcontrol harms both the illegal employment of foreign workers (beneficial to many employers) and the equal treatment of Belgian and migrant workers (the goal of the unions). Nevertheless, this behavior is predominantly (but not exclusively) subordinate to the interests of the class that dominates the government organization in question.[4]

Another simplification concerns the delineation of class interests. First, not all capitalist entrepreneurs are interested in the availability of cheap foreign labor in Belgian labor markets. Indeed, many entrepreneurs do not need that foreign labor reserve and would rather see their taxes drop than have tax money used to provide immigrants with some elementary social and cultural accommodations. The availability of cheap foreign labor is demanded, however, by a large number of enterprises in most sectors of the economy. Therefore, it is retained here as the most important capitalist class interest at stake in the immigration policy struggle. (Nevertheless, no fraction of capital wants to see an oversupply of immigrant labor because of the tax costs and threat of social unrest.)

Second, there is the union's goal, which is already a compromise between the fundamental opposition of the unions against immigration and their attitude regarding economic decision making in general – that is, to leave the initiative for production and for organization of the work process in the hands of private capitalist entrepreneurs. The unions are opposed to immigration because it means a threat to the income level, the work circumstances, and even to the job security of domestic workers. The unions are afraid that, if migrant workers overflow the domestic labor markets, they will be prepared to work under worse conditions than the Belgians would tolerate. However, the unions take for granted the capitalist production initiative, which makes the mass importation of foreign workers unavoidable. This explains the unions' compromise, which is their demand for equal and improved rights for both domestic and foreign workers.

The Work Permit Process: The Government as Gatekeeper

The intervention of the government with respect to the employment of foreign workers in Belgium rests on the following formal process negotiated in the ARI:[5]

1. Employers initiate the hiring process. They can only employ a foreigner if they have obtained permission from the Ministry of Employment and Labor and as soon as the foreigner himself (herself) disposes of a work permit.
2. The Minister will grant his permission to the employer and the work permit to the foreigner only after an examination of the local labor market. At present, this examination responsibility rests with the RVA (the National Service for Work Provision). The number of unemployed workers or vacant labor positions is often decisive in this examination.

3. The first permit (B permit) is temporary and obliges the foreigner to stay with the same employer for one year and to stay in the same sector for two or three years. After this period, the foreigner can apply for an automatic, unlimited-duration permit (A permit) and can freely choose employer and sector.
4. The government recognizes the right of family reunion. This means that the foreign spouse and the children of the head of the family who is employed in Belgium are also allowed to come to stay in Belgium. The members of the family can obtain A permits as soon as the head of the family has obtained an A permit. The application of the principle of family reunion thus leads to new, induced immigration flows.

The government, in controlling the migration flows, plays only the role of a gatekeeper. The government can control only the direct flows of migrant workers – the flows that are initiated by the employers (B permits). The government must automatically grant the legally allowed family reunion (A permits) unless the law is changed.[6]

From the history of immigration policy, we learn that, in case of shortages in the labor markets, the role of gatekeeper is reduced to the role of a mere spectator. When unemployment is high, however, that role becomes more significant; the government applies the work and residence regulations very strictly and looks for possible limitations of the right of family reunion and for measures to intensify police control.

The Historical Development of Belgian Immigration Policy

The State

Before the 1930s, when the employment of migrant workers was not yet dependent on any legal regulation, the employment of a foreign worker was subject to a private agreement between the migrant and the employer. Since the 1930s, especially with the approval of the KB (royal decree) of March 31, 1936, both parties had to receive preliminary permission from the Minister of Labor. The validity of the work permit was limited with respect to the nature, the place, and the duration of employment. The transaction between foreign worker and employer thus became the object of governmental intervention. The refusal or the permission was mainly dependent on the domestic unemployment situation – that is, whether any domestic labor force was available.

There was no kind of institutionalized negotiation between the government, the employers' organizations, and the workers' organizations until 1948, when ministerial departments and employers' and workers' organizations started reciprocity consultation. This consultation, first in the DCVA, later in the ARI,[7] dealt with the following items:

1. The granting of contingents of foreign workers to certain enterprises;
2. The yearly determination of the criteria to obtain a work permit (for example, preference measures, privileged sectors);
3. The application of the law, especially of Article 3 of the KB of March 22, 1936, regarding the granting of a work permit before immigration.[8]

From 1948 to 1967, the approval or refusal of contingents and the yearly determination of the criteria to obtain a work permit were the main points of discussion at the DCVA and later at the ARI. Until 1962–1963, government functionaries at the DCVA were in a position to arbitrate between the delegations of workers and employers. Although the DCVA merely advised the Minister of Employment, the final decision by the Minister almost always coincided with DCVA recommendations.

After 1963 the ministerial departments (especially the Ministries of Employment and Labor, Justice, and Foreign Affairs) took a more independent stance toward the development of immigration policy. A number of factors were at the basis of this weakening of the negotiation process in the DCVA/ARI. First, the acceptance of spontaneous tourist immigration (1963–1967) made discussions about the granting of work permits and the determination of criteria for contingents superfluous. Second, the flood of tourist-workers meant that reception, adaptation, integration, and assimilation of foreigners became more pressing items on the agenda of the DCVA than did negotiating numbers of immigrants.[9] In fact, the mandate of the DCVA was redefined to include advice regarding "all social, economic and administrative problems set by immigration."[10] Finally, the employment of migrant workers became governed increasingly by international regulations and agreements (for example, the free circulation of EEC workers in EEC countries). The freedom of national political decisions in migration matters was increasingly limited.

The joint effect of these different factors is that negotiation and policy-setting activities in the ARI – the union's major voice in the State – have weakened significantly. In reaction to the severe employment crisis of 1974, the government pronounced a halt to immigration, legalized all illegally employed foreign workers, and strengthened controls to prevent illegal employment.[11] This led to a tightened control of migrants in Belgium, a step backward in the domestic liberalization of the labor markets for migrants. Even the strengthening of sanctions against employers of illegal migrants[12] could not prevent foreigners – the important absentees in the immigration debate – from becoming the first victims of the measures of August 1, 1974. Thus, these changes meant a direct setback for union efforts to develop equal rights for immigrants.

The Employers

To stimulate the supply of unskilled workers, employers have tried to promote the recruiting of workers abroad. As early as 1937, Belgian mine bosses began this practice. In agreement with different Ministries (Foreign Affairs, Labor, Economic Affairs), recruitment missions were sent abroad. After World War II, this practice was generalized.[13] The production of coal was considered so essential to the reconstruction of the economy that the government decided to help mine bosses as much as they could, so that the importation of labor power could happen under optimal circumstances. As we have seen, however, employers in other sectors soon discovered the benefits of having access to foreign labor reserves and tried to obtain preferential treatment for their enterprises or sectors (that is, special recruitment systems). They objected to measures that set bounds to immigration. In order to reduce recruitment costs caused by the contingent system, they insisted that spontaneous tourist immigration be allowed. They argued that selection and legalization could be done more easily in Belgium.

At the same time, employers were far from enthusiastic when, through the introduction of the A permit, the obligation for a migrant to work for a certain time in the same enterprise or sector was relaxed or abolished. This type of internal liberalization of the labor market, which might make employers lose their control of foreign personnel, was not appreciated very much. Even after the restriction of immigration, first in 1967 and again in 1974, employers successfully went on demanding immigration when necessary.[14]

The Unions

It was not until March 1948 that the Belgian trade unions demanded negotiation rights with respect to immigration policy. The direct cause for this demand was increasing unemployment and the fact "that foreign labor could become a dangerous competitor for Belgian workers."[15] The unions tried to maintain (or regain) their monopoly on the supply of labor. They tried to avoid any competition between groups of workers, which could be exploited by employers through lower wages or worse working conditions. For this purpose, the unions fought at two levels. At the external level, they fought to prevent large groups of foreigners from overflowing the Belgian labor markets. Therefore, the demand by employers for contingents of foreign workers had to be driven back, and *post factum* regularization of already employed foreign tourists had to be discouraged. At the internal level, the unions fought to discourage employers from hiring large groups of foreigners. Therefore, the cost of indigenous and foreign labor had to be the same. That is why the unions have always demanded equal treatment in wages, working time, social security, and so forth.

However, unions demanded participation not only in employment problems but also in other problems of national economic policy: the viability of enterprises and economic sectors, price policy, the competitive position of the national economy, and so on. Because inflows of foreign labor can ameliorate these other national problems, the unions, as soon as they considered themselves responsible for the smooth functioning of the national economy, also had to accept that, under certain circumstances, the employment of foreign workers was necessary.[16]

Primarily, the unions were against labor immigration during economic downturns. To be sure that foreigners would not enter into competition with Belgian workers, the unions requested guarantees that would limit the number of work permits granted during periods of high unemployment. These guarantees could be granted with the agreement of the union delegates, or Works Council, and the DCVA (later the ARI). In general, these measures come down to a strict application of the work permit laws, for both employer and worker. It should be noted that restricting labor migration during slack periods is also in the interest of employers, who want to avoid the high taxes and social unrest associated with large pools of unemployed workers.

For the last few years, the unions have defended a so-called structural immigration policy, linked to the social, political, and cultural integration of foreigners already living in Belgium. In a policy-advice note, the ACV/CSC (Christian Union) recommends no further immigration so long as employers are not willing to meet their demands for equal rights for foreign workers.[17] The ACV/CSC points out that Belgium should avoid investing in activities that require large quantities of unskilled labor and night-shift work. Moreover, the ACV/CSC, which, in principle, is a strong proponent of stopping immigration in the long run, defends a number of measures to be taken in the short run: unambiguous guarantees for housing, taxation of the recruitment of migrants, the reform of administrative and penal sanctions for illegal employment, and an intensification of work control.[18] The ACV/CSC defends a halt to immigration as the only effective pressure on employers to improve working conditions. However, it realizes that such a halt can be executed only in the long run, because, if introduced too suddenly, it would cause severe bottlenecks for many enterprises.

Whose Immigration Policy Is This?

In table 10-1 the opposed class interests at stake in the struggle for an appropriate immigration policy have been translated into concrete goals. In addition, the table indicates the instruments that both parties want the state to use and the relative success or failure by which their goals are achieved in two extreme situations: shortages on most labor markets — so-called full employment — and high unemployment.

In both situations, employers' organizations have seen their goals attained — even without the functioning of free migration under high unemployment. Here, in fact, the employers benefit from the unions' actions for the right to family reunion and the right to an A permit. For the unions, these actions were meant as steps toward the acquisition of equal rights for migrants and Belgians. They had an unintended byproduct, however; they led to an induced supply of foreign workers and hence helped provide employers with a sufficiently large reserve of unskilled workers.

The unions, on the other hand, have scored poorly with respect to both their goals. It is true that unions have had some success with their actions for equal rights for migrants and Belgians. However, some basic discrimination in the sphere of social security and legal and political rights remains, and no substantial progress has been made for the last fifteen years. The only goal that has received an unambiguous positive score is the limitation of supply under high unemployment, because it does not interfere with the employers' goal of an assured supply of unskilled labor force. Moreover, the limitation of supply has led to increased control and oppression of the migrants in the country. Although the unions are against this control and favor control at the borders of the country, they could not prevent it. Moreover, the present situation of high unemployment produced a partial abolishment of existing rights for migrants (such as the right of family reunion) — a setback for the second goal.

Statistical Analysis of the Permit-Granting Policy, (1961–1979)

One of the important conclusions of the previous sections is that the employers' position has been dominant in the conception of an immigration policy and that, as a consequence, the laws and regulations that form the legal

Table 10-1. How Successful Are Social Partners in Immigration Policy?

		Full Employment	*High Unemployment*
Employers			
Goals	1. Assure supply of unskilled labor power	+ +	+
	2. Restrict internal freedom of movement of foreign workers	+	+ +
Instruments	1. Free immigration	+	−
	2. Selection and regularization in Belgium	+	+
Unions			
Goals	1. Limit supply of unskilled labor power in function of economic needs	−	+
	2. Equal rights for migrant and Belgian workers	− +	−
Instruments	1. Strict application of work permit laws	−	+
	2. Oppose regularization	−	−
	3. Social laws and regulations	+ −	− +

Key: + = goal achieved or instrument used; − = goal unachieved or instrument not used; double sign means stress.

base for the granting of work permits have been developed in a way that makes it easy to provide the domestic labor markets with foreign labor power or to clear them when needed. An empirical examination of actual work permits granted over time substantiates the point that government actions have regulated the flow of immigrants to match employers' needs.[19] Also, a sectoral analysis of the permits granted reinforces the point that services have shown the greatest relative growth in demand for low-wage, low-skilled immigrant labor.

Although they are indicative, however, the results are not conclusive. Total demand for foreign labor power – as compared to the demand actually met by work permits – cannot be estimated. Also, the number of work permits granted does not reflect total supply of immigrant labor because of (1) illegal workers and (2) the fact that workers from other EEC countries no longer needed a work permit after 1967. Consequently, we can only examine whether the evolution of the numbers of work permits assigned follows the general fluctuations in the business cycle and long-term growth trends (or, in Belgium, stagnation trends), and what the sectoral composition of permits granted – rather than workers demanded – has been.

It must also be pointed out that the government does not have complete control over the number of permits granted. Almost half of the first work permits (that is, nonrenewals) granted between 1961 and 1967 were A permits that went to applicants who had already worked for a number of years in the country or who requested a family reunion. These permits are permanent. Since 1967, 80 percent of the first work permits have been A permits.

The results of the actual statistical analysis of the dynamic trends in discretionary permits granted show that the frequency of the cycle of the number of assigned permits follows that of the business cycle very well. Before the 1970s, however, the amplitude of the work permit cycle was in disproportion with the amplitude of the business cycle. In fact, the changes in employment of foreign workers find only a poor statistical explanation in the business cycle fluctuations. They do, however, show a strong correlation with the stagnating growth path of the Belgian economy after 1970.

A sectoral analysis of 1961 to 1979 shows that, of the total of all work permits granted for particular sectors (282,730 permits), 19 percent were granted for the metal industry, 10 percent for the coal mines, 13 percent for personal services, 10 percent for the construction sector, 7 percent for textile and clothing, and 7 percent for trade, banking and insurance. Together, these sectors are responsible for over 70 percent of the total number of the first-granted work permits.

In order to interpret these sectoral data in due order, one should take into account not only the difference between modes of granting (with or without immigration) and the kind of work permit (A or B), but also their intertemporal evolution. According to the mode of granting and the kind of work permit, a clear distinction can be seen between the sectors of employment. Such a distinction becomes very clear when comparing the granting of first-year B permits with immigration (neither freedom of choice nor mobility of the migrant worker is allowed) and the first A permits without immigration (freedom of choice and some preliminary knowledge of the labor market). Workers with a first B permit with immigration had as their main sectors of destination coal mines, metal industry, construction, and personal services, whereas the induced supply (A permits without immigration) found itself in the metal industry, personal services, clothing, and trade, banking, and insurance.

The share of A permits in the number of permits at immigration is very high in the sectors involving foodstuffs, clothing, miscellaneous industries, and services of general interest. The share of B permits at immigration in the number of first permits is extremely high in agriculture, mining, quarries, chemicals, construction, and low-skilled services (hotels, restaurants, transportation and traffic, services to persons). All these latter activities are known for their poor working conditions in one respect or another, which might explain why they rely strongly on new foreign labor power, that is, directly imported from abroad and without immediate family connections.

As to the sectoral distribution of the work permits at immigration over time (see figure 10-1), the shares of business services (particularly general services, and trade, banking, and insurance) have increased the most significantly, along with chemicals, the metal industry, and transportation, while the shares of mining, textile, nonmetallic mineral industry, and construction have fallen sharply. Sectors with near-constant shares are services to persons and the foodstuffs industry. Similarly, the halt to immigration in 1974, which reduced the total number of granted work permits, was felt the least in general services.

We can conclude that the numbers of assigned work permits and their distribution over the different sectors have followed the general pattern of stagnation and tertiarization that has characterized employment in the Belgian economy for the last decade. The point of gravity of new employment has shifted from industry to services, particularly business and financial services; yet the use of immigrant labor in traditional industries typified by poor working conditions has remained high. We learned in another study, however, that the shift from industry to services by immigrants has not been as spectacular as the same shift in the Belgian labor force.[20] This is because the restructuring of industry and the prolongation of the life of old, traditional industrial activities has made relatively more use of poorly qualified workers (including a large proportion of migrants) than of highly qualified workers.[21]

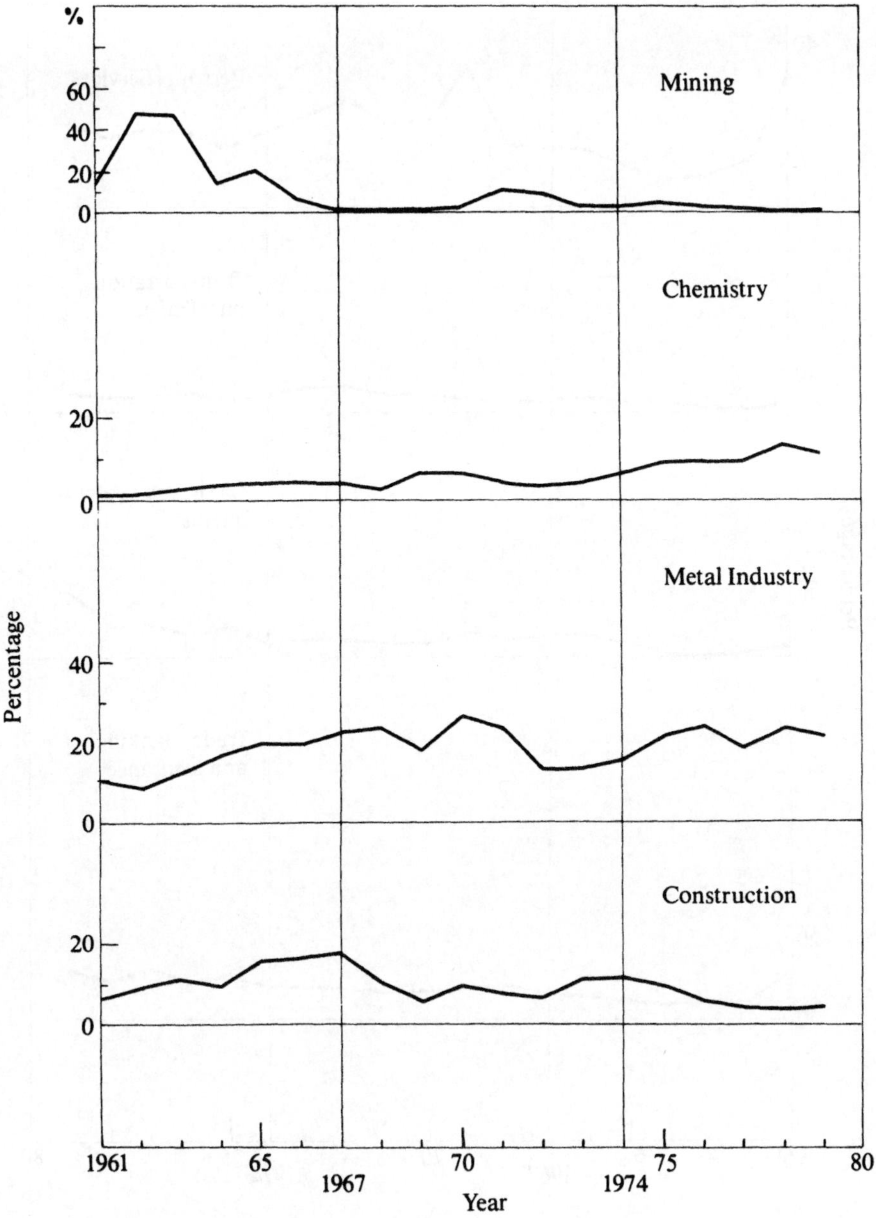

FIGURE 10-1. SECTORAL SHARE IN TOTAL NUMBER OF GRANTED FIRST-YEAR WORK PERMITS (A AND B PERMITS AT IMMIGRATION)

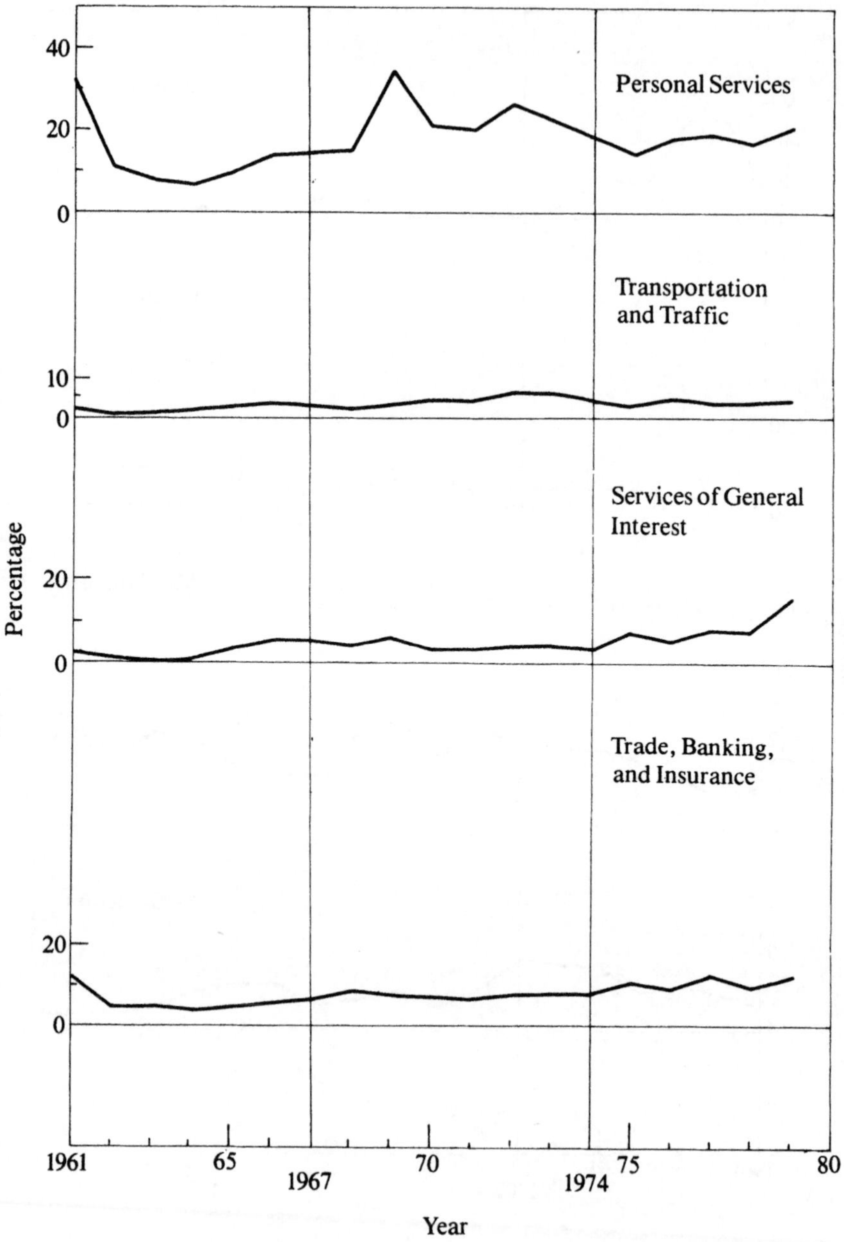

FIGURE 10-1. SECTORAL SHARE IN TOTAL NUMBER OF GRANTED FIRST-YEAR WORK PERMITS (CONTINUED)

Conclusion

The State has indeed been an arena for expressing the conflict between capital and labor over immigration policy. It has not been a responsive arena for the unions' positions for two main reasons: (1) the economic and political strength of the employers' organizations and (2) the contradictory goals of the unions – a halt to immigration versus equal rights for immigrants versus a voice in national economic policy to promote capital accumulation.

Industrial restructuring, especially the lowering of job skill requirements that accompanies the new international division of labor, has put the unions in a position of having to defend the quality of work available to them, yet it has provided them with no viable strategies to do so. Until the flow of low-skilled migrants who are willing to accept low-paying jobs is cut off, the unions will have little bargaining power over the quality of work for domestic and migrant workers in Belgium. Because the State has proved to be an unresponsive bargaining arena, unions must incorporate a strategy of direct negotiations with employers over the organization of work.

Notes

1. The tendency toward lowering skill requirements of jobs has been perceived by Conen and Huijgen (1980) in the Netherlands and by Freyssenet (1973) in a number of industries in France. Conen and Huijgen measured the share of the interesting professions in the different sectors of the Dutch economy and found that, on the average, this share has diminished between 1961 and 1970. Unfortunately, no similar research has been undertaken for the Belgian economy; but the partial results obtained from the study of indirect indicators (such as the shares of migrants and women in blue-collar employment) point to the existence of a similar dequalification phenomenon (see, for example, Martens and Moulaert 1982).

2. For a number of basic references on the theory of the State, see chapter 4.

3. Migrant organizations estimated the number of illegal workers in April 1974 at twenty to forty thousand.

4. Examples of autonomous interventions by the State Security and the Foreigners' Police are given in the Flemish weekly *De Nieuwe*, 1973 to 1976.

5. These principles have been translated into many Laws and Orders in Council (KBs). For an exhaustive list, see Martens and Moulaert (1981).

6. See, among others, the KBs of October 5, 1979, including modifications of the KBs of July 20 and November 6, 1967.

7. The Tripartite Commission for Foreign Labor Force (DCVA) was convoked for the first time on July 12, 1948, after the first National Labor Conference (March 30, 1948). In 1965, the DCVA was replaced by the Advisory Council for Immigration, ARI (inaugurated by KB on August 12, 1965). Like the DCVA, the ARI is an advisory organ to the Minister of Employment and Labor, but its jurisdiction is extended to examine all problems caused by immigration.

8. In periods of shortages in labor markets, the government authorities drop the preliminary admission procedure. Migrants can be employed without work permits and their situation can be regularized *post factum*. Moreover, they are not bothered by the Foreigners' Police.

9. For the demographic aspects of Belgian immigration policy, see Martens (1976, p. 26ff).

10. Such advice was formulated by the National Action for Social Security, "De immigratie-en onthaalpolitiek der buitenlandse werknemers in Belgie" (Brussels, mimeographed, 1977).

11. See the Law of July 22, 1976, modifying KB Nr. 34 of July 20, 1967, regarding the employment of workers of foreign nationality and the Law of June 30, 1971, regarding administrative fines applicable in case of infraction of certain social laws. *Belgisch Staatsblad* (1976).

12. See Moulaert (1979, p. 822).

13. A large number of bilateral agreements have been concluded between inmigration and outmigration nations. In principle, only citizens of a nation with which a labor force agreement has been concluded can come to work in Belgium. By way of exception, Belgium allows political refugees, spouse and children with a foreign nationality, and individual migrants to come work here, even when they fall outside the scope of a labor force agreement.

The recruitment is done in the outmigration country itself, where the selection takes place and where the work contract is signed. All this happens without the migrant's knowledge of the employer and the nature of the work. Such a recruitment at the source allows selection of the most valuable labor force from an ample supply. The recruitment criteria are usually enumerated in the agreement texts; there are prerequisites regarding age (for example, only workers between 20 and 35 years of age are eligible), qualifications, police record, and health. Before they leave their country, migrants must undergo a medical examination, which is repeated upon their arrival in Belgium.

For a list of bilateral conventions and a more in-depth evaluation, see Moulaert and Declerck (1975). See, also, Bollen and Moulaert (1982).

14. In 1967, the government began to apply the law again. This meant that tourist migration and *post factum* regularization were no longer allowed. From then on, foreign, non-EEC workers could be employed only if they had work permits.

15. See Evalenko (1968).

16. This is stated very explicitly in the working document, "Verantwoordelijk voor de toekonst," for the Twenty-fourth Congress of the ACV, the Christian Union, on October 24–26, 1968: "Foreign workers are no 'cheap labor reserve' in our economic policy... In positive terms this means we are in favor of an organized and integral immigration policy which reconciles the right to emigrate alone and with family, with the economy and the demography of the host country" (p. 194).

17. See Confederation des Syndicats Chretiens (1975).

18. Moulaert (1979) explains that the demands by the unions that are effectively met (uniform penal and administrative sanctions, limitation of immigration) tighten the qualitative controls but do not hinder the necessary quantitative supplies of foreign workers. Concrete measures to give foreign workers and their families equal rights – politically, socially, and culturally – have only seldom been taken.

19. An alternative would have been to compare statistically the evolution per sector of the number of unfilled vacancies with the number of attributed work permits. In this way, one could check whether a correlation exists between the number of unfilled vacancies and the number of foreigners entering the labor markets. Unfortunately, the data of unfilled vacancies published by the RVA (the official employment office) are too partial to be useful for such a correlation analysis.

20. See Martens and Moulaert (1982).

21. See Moulaert (1981).

References

Bollen, R., and Moulaert, F. 1982. *Racisten hebben ongelijk* [Racists are wrong]. Leuven, Belgium: Kritak.

Conen, G., and Huijgen, F. 1980. "De kwalitatieve structuur van de werkgelegenheid in 1960 en 1971 (1)" [The qualitative structure of employment in 1960 and 1971]. *Economisch Statistische Berichten,* pp. 480–487.

Confédération des Syndicats Chrétiens. 1975. "Propositions de la C.S.C. en matière de politique d'immigration." Doc. 75/64. Brussels.

Evalenko, R. 1968. *Régime économique de la Belgique.* Brussels-Leuven: Vanler.

Freyssenet, M. 1973. *La division capitaliste du travail.* Paris: Savelli.

Martens, A. 1976. *Le Immigrés, Flux et reflux d'une main-d'oeuvre d'appoint.* Louvain: Presses Universitaires de Louvain.

Martens, A. and Moulaert, F. 1981. "Het immigratiebeleid van de Belgische Overheid" [The Immigration Policy of the Belgian Government]. *Referaten van het XVe Vlaams Wetenschappelijk Economisch Congres.* Leuven: Vereniging voor Economie, May, pp. 133–145.

Martens, A., and Moulaert, F. 1982. "Production, Emploi et Immigration" [Production, Employment and Immigration]. *Contradictions,* in press.

Moulaert, F. 1979. "Wiens immigratiebeleid is dit?" *De Gids op Maatschappelijk Gebied,* pp. 819–835.

______. 1981. "Economic Crisis and the Employment of Foreign Workers in the Belgian Economy." *Studies in Comparative International Development,* (Summer), pp. 47–66.

Moulaert, F., and Declerck, J. 1975. "De Gastarbeid in de Europese Gemeenschap" [Migrant Labor in the EEC]. *Tijdschrift voor Diplomatie* (October).

Moulaert, F., and Philips, F. 1982. "The Employment of Migrant Workers in the Belgian Economy: A Structural Phenomenon." *Environment and Planning A.*

LIST OF CONTRIBUTORS

David Barkin
Professor of Economics
Universidad Autonoma Metropolitana
Mexico

Robert B. Cohen
Senior Research Associate
Conservation of Human Resources
Columbia University
New York

Jose Luis Coraggio
Regional Planner
Organization of American States
Nicaragua

Panagis Liossatos
Professor of Economics
Florida International University
Miami

Ann R. Markusen
Assistant Professor of Urban and Regional Planning
University of California
Berkeley

Frank Moulaert
Researcher
Centrum voor Economische Studiën
Katholieke Universiteit
Leuven, Belgium

Thierry J. Noyelle
Research Associate
Conservation of Human Resources
Columbia University
New York

Patricia Wilson Salinas
Assistant Professor
Graduate Program of Community and Regional Planning
University of Texas
Austin

INDEX

This index is a survey of *concepts* used in regional political economy. Proper names are mentioned only to indicate the concrete spatial phenomena to which the concepts have been applied.

GPSR Compliance

The European Union's (EU) General Product Safety Regulation (GPSR) is a set of rules that requires consumer products to be safe and our obligations to ensure this.

If you have any concerns about our products, you can contact us on ProductSafety@springernature.com

In case Publisher is established outside the EU, the EU authorized representative is:

Springer Nature Customer Service Center GmbH
Europaplatz 3
69115 Heidelberg, Germany

Batch number: 10830943

Printed by Printforce, the Netherlands